A Tale of Two Midwives

A new town, a new hospital—and new connections?

Best friends Grace and Jenni have sworn off romance. They adore bringing little miracles into the world, but their jobs as midwives are as close to love and babies as they're going to get. Until fate leads them across the globe and straight into the arms of the men who'll change everything...

Falling for Her Forbidden Flatmate

Living with her best friend's brother might not be ideal, but after a difficult divorce, a fresh start in New Zealand is just what Grace needs. What she could do without is the undeniable chemistry between her and gorgeous obstetrician Jock... Giving in to their attraction would be a terrible idea. But will she be able to resist her roommate?

Miracle Twins to Heal Them

On the last night of her trip to visit Grace and Jock, Jenni finds herself alone with deliciously handsome anesthetist Dan. But what was supposed to be a vacation fling becomes oh-so-complicated when she discovers that she's pregnant—with *twins*!

Both available now!

Dear Reader,

I was born and bred and now live in the South Island of New Zealand, and we like to call ourselves the Mainlanders ;-) In an amazing country overall, the South Island has more than its fair share of attractions and, if you're ever lucky enough to get here, don't miss the top. The Marlborough Sounds are stunning and that's where my twin siblings—Jock, the hero of *Falling for Her Forbidden Flatmate*, and Jenni, the heroine of *Miracle Twins to Heal Them*—end up living.

Their shared childhood had scarred them both badly enough that they were in danger of missing out on the best that life can offer—true love.

Fortunately, Grace and Dan come into their lives, and it's not just the scenery that will take their breath away.

Happy reading.

With love,

Alison xxx

FALLING FOR HER FORBIDDEN FLATMATE

ALISON ROBERTS

Harlequin

MEDICAL ROMANCE

Harlequin®
MEDICAL
ROMANCE

ISBN-13: 978-1-335-94256-2

Falling for Her Forbidden Flatmate

Harlequin Enterprises ULC
22 Adelaide St. West, 41st Floor
Toronto, Ontario M5H 4E3, Canada
www.Harlequin.com

Printed in U.S.A.

Recycling programs for this product may not exist in your area.

Alison Roberts has been lucky enough to live in the South of France for several years recently but is now back in her home country of New Zealand. She is also lucky enough to write for the Harlequin Medical Romance line. A primary school teacher in a former life, she later became a qualified paramedic. She loves to travel and dance, drink champagne, and spend time with her daughter and her friends. Alison is the author of over one hundred books!

PROLOGUE

IT WAS THE noise that made her turn her head, but it was what she thought she could see that made the chill run down Grace's spine like a trickle of ice-cold water—so shocking it made her gasp.

'What's wrong, Grace?'

'Did you see that?'

'What?'

'I think someone was looking in our window.'

'You're not sure?'

Grace frowned. It had almost been more of a feeling than anything visual. 'I just saw something out of the corner of my eye and then it was gone…'

As if someone had moved fast because they didn't want to be seen?

'It was probably just a branch on that tree in the street moving. This storm's moving in fast. Listen to the wind and rain—who'd be mad enough to go out in this just to look through people's windows?' Jenni smiled. 'And how good is it that we've both had the day off and we can stay warm and dry?'

But then Jenni's brow creased with concern.

'You've been jumpy ever since we heard that gossip about your ex. News that comes through any hospital grapevine should always be taken with a grain of salt, you know.'

'I know. And you're right. I'm just on edge.' Grace blew out a steadying breath as she got up from the couch. Perhaps physically moving would quell the upside-down sensation in her stomach? 'Why should it bother me anyway? I'm not surprised wife number two has walked out on him.'

She knew exactly why it would have happened and it was too hard to not have memories trying to escape the place where she'd done her best to lock them away. That could well be the reason she'd imagined something menacing lurking in the shadows.

Grace moved swiftly to the windows and pulled the curtains closed, shutting out the darkness. It was only late afternoon but the days were short and could be bleak in the tail end of a Scottish winter.

The small gas fire was providing welcome warmth indoors but Jenni, her flatmate, who was curled up on one end of the couch with a laptop open on her knees, still had a blanket draped around her shoulders.

'Come and look at this, Grace. Jock's sent some more photos.'

A distraction was exactly what was needed. Grace sat beside her friend, picking up a corner of the blanket so it was around both of them. Maybe this was what she really needed—to remind herself that moving all the way from London to Glasgow to do her midwifery training had been the best thing she'd ever done, because she'd met Jenni, who was her best friend ever and now they lived together and worked at the same maternity hospital and...

...and Grace was finally starting to feel genuinely safe for the first time in far too long.

'Oh...'

The sound was one of longing because what Grace was seeing on the screen was so idyllic. A deep blue sea that was calm enough to be reflecting the rugged-looking hills of the nearby tree-covered islands. A sky that was as blue as the sea with not a cloud to be seen. The photo had been taken looking over the stern of a small boat.

'And look at this...' Jenni clicked on the arrow.

The next image had a pod of dolphins following the boat, leaping over the foam of the wake. It made Grace smile.

'They look *so* happy, don't they? I love dolphins.'

'Jock's just as happy. He says it's paradise. Mostly...'

'Only mostly? Just how fussy is your brother?'

'Apparently they're so short of midwives that he's having to do some perfectly normal deliveries himself and he says he didn't train to be an obstetrician for so many years just to catch babies.' Jenni shook her head. 'He says it's messing with his love life and his fishing, and that wasn't part of the plan when he moved to New Zealand.' She closed the laptop. 'I think he's sending me all these postcard pictures to try and entice me to go and join him. He even took photos of all the spare bedrooms in the house that's available for hospital staff.'

'And you're not tempted?' Grace could hear the wind rattling the window in this tiny living room of the terraced house they shared. At least, she *hoped* it was the wind...

'It's a tiny little town at the top of the South Island. Almost a village, and I'm never going to live in a place that small again. You couldn't have a night out without the entire town knowing about it, and where's the fun if you can't meet anyone new, anyway?'

Grace shook her head. 'Didn't you say that Jock seems to find a new girlfriend every other week or so?'

'True. The only long-term commitment he's going to make won't be to any woman. It'll be to that boat he's bought. Going out fishing is his favourite thing to do.' Jenni shuddered. 'I hate boats. I fell out of one once, when I was about seven or eight. Jock will deny it, but he totally pushed me.'

'I thought twins were supposed to be lifelong soul mates?'

'He thought it was funny.' Jenni was smiling now. 'It kind of was, I guess. It was summer and we were living in a place that had a huge pond. One of the better foster homes we got sent to because we got to stay together.' Her tone was overly bright. 'Want to get something delivered for dinner? Like a pizza with the crust that's stuffed full of cheese?'

'Sounds good.' Grace knew when a subject needed to be changed. She pulled out her phone. 'What's the name of the town where Jock works?'

'Picton. It's where the ferries go in and out, getting from the North Island to the South Island. They have to go through the Marlborough Sounds, which have hundreds of islands which are apparently the tops of an ancient mountain range that sank into the sea.'

'And it's got a hospital big enough to need an obstetrician and midwives?'

'I think it covers quite a big population but it's spread out. Some of the islands are inhabited. Jock says that sometimes the midwives have to go to home visits or deliveries by boat.'

Grace was scrolling through more images on her phone. 'It looks amazing.'

'It's totally on the other side of the world. Who on earth would want to go there? Unless you were really into boats, of course.'

Grace glanced up—towards the windows, where a draught was making the curtains billow gently. 'I can think of other reasons the other side of the world might be a good place to live,' she said quietly. 'It would make it a lot harder for someone to find you, wouldn't it?'

Jenni was silent for a moment. 'Well, Jock would be thrilled if you wanted to apply for a job there. I'd miss you like crazy, but—'

'But you'd *have* to come and visit, wouldn't you?' Grace interrupted. 'You've been saying for ages that you must go and visit Jock one of these days.'

Jenni blinked. 'You really *like* the idea, don't you?'

'I wouldn't want to live with your brother, mind you. He sounds like he thinks any single woman is fair game.'

'Hey…if I told him you were out of bounds you'd be as safe as houses. Apart from you, Jock is the only person on earth that I would trust with my life.'

There was a much longer silence this time. One that was full of things that hadn't been spoken about since a night of wine-fuelled confessions between two new best friends. Stories of children who had never been wanted and a woman who'd been trapped in a desperately unhappy situation. The bonding of two women who'd learned that courage and determination could get them where they wanted to go.

But they both knew, all too well, that it was dangerous to assume nothing else could go wrong.

'You know I'll support you whatever you want to do,' Jenni said quietly. 'But do you really think he would come looking for you? Just because he's single again?'

Grace didn't answer because her phone was vibrating in her hand. She closed the webpage but didn't answer the call. Instead, she held the screen so that Jenni could see the message that said *No caller ID.*

It was most likely one of those automated calls from a scammer but Grace felt another one of those shivers run down her spine as she caught Jenni's gaze. Her fingers moving to find the setting that would block the caller.

'Probably not,' she said softly. 'But the real problem is that I'm thinking about it again. I'm not going to let that happen. And if making a fresh start on the other side of the planet is what it takes, then that's what I'll do.'

CHAPTER ONE

IT FELT AS if Grace Collins had stepped into one of those postcard images that Jock had sent to his twin sister on that stormy night in Glasgow.

Good grief...was it only five or six weeks ago?

Picton Hospital had clearly been desperate enough for a new midwife to arrive that they'd accelerated the online interview process and all the paperwork needed for her to be able to work in a new country.

And here she was, in the early hours of the first day in her new life, sailing between the islands towards the pretty seaside town that was going to be her new home. It still didn't feel real but part of that had to be jetlag, despite getting a decent amount of sleep on the long haul from Glasgow to Wellington. It was good that she'd chosen a ferry trip rather than a quick flight on a small plane to cross the strait between the islands because it was giving her a bit of breathing space to get used to the speed with which her life was changing.

Passengers who didn't have a vehicle to take off

the ferry were allowed to disembark first. Grace rolled her suitcase along the wharf, found a taxi with a friendly driver who even took a bit of a detour to show her where the hospital was and, in no time at all, she was bumping her case up the concrete steps of an old villa. She took a deep breath at the top of the steps, looked over her shoulder to a stunning view of a marina with a forest of yacht masts and a backdrop of the sea and islands and found she was smiling as she reached for an old iron door knocker to announce her arrival.

Her smile began to fade, however, as the door was opened a few seconds later by a woman with tousled blonde hair. She had a piece of toast in one hand with a large bite taken out of a corner and she was wearing a man's shirt that only had the lowest buttons fastened. It was quite clear that she wasn't wearing anything at all underneath the shirt.

Grace blinked. 'Um… I'm Grace,' she said. 'This is the hospital accommodation, isn't it?'

'Yeah…' The woman's smile was as friendly as the taxi driver's had been. 'Jock said someone might be arriving this morning. Come in.' She pulled the door open wider, turning to look down the long hallway. 'Jock? Are you out of bed yet?'

'No need to shout, Greta.'

The man who came through one of the doors opening onto the hallway was, thankfully, wearing more clothes than Greta. He might have bare feet and spiky, unbrushed hair but his faded denim jeans and tee shirt were perfectly respectable for a late Sunday morning and she would have recognised Jock McKay anywhere. With his red hair, bright blue eyes and freckled pale skin he was the male equivalent of Jenni and that made it feel as if she knew him already. His smile was far cheekier than Jenni's, however, and he had the confidence of a man who never had the slightest difficulty charming any woman he chose to.

Even Grace, who was immune to any male charm being directed at her, found herself smiling back at him.

'You're just in time for breakfast,' he told her. Then his smile widened. 'Or maybe that should be brunch? Can I tempt you to one of my famous bacon butties?'

His accent was just as familiar as his looks and the warmth of that smile just as welcoming as the offer of food. Grace had to blink back a sudden prickle behind her eyes that threatened—embarrassingly—to turn into tears.

She was tired, that was all. Jetlagged and displaced and suddenly on the wrong side of the world and winter had become summer but…

…but it felt, astonishingly, like she'd finally arrived home.

* * *

Wow...

Jock McKay had seen pictures of Grace Collins with his sister over the last few years but they hadn't done justice at all to the woman now sitting on one of the wicker chairs in the shade of the veranda which was one of the best features of this old house. Grace was eating the bacon sandwich he'd made for her after she'd had a chance to put her suitcase in her bedroom and freshen up.

His date from last night, Greta, had gone to start her day's work in one of the town's popular pubs and it was no hardship for Jock to spend a bit of time to make his sister's best friend feel welcome.

'Is that good?'

'Best buttie ever.' Grace licked a drop of smoky barbecue sauce from her fingers. 'Jenni didn't tell me you could cook.'

'It's a recently acquired splinter skill.' Jock grinned. 'I had to learn to do something with the fish I was catching so I made friends with a frying pan.'

'Ah... I saw photos of your boat. It's cute. Wooden?'

'Her name's *Lassie*. And aye, she's a clinker cabin cruiser.'

'Did you name her?'

'No. She was already a Scottish boat. That was how I knew it was meant to be.'

'Does she have sails or a motor?'

'Both, but I tend to use the motor more. It's one with a propellor so she's not as fast as a jet boat, but who wants to hurry when you're out in the Sounds? It's the most beautiful place on earth.'

Grace was nodding. 'I loved coming in on the ferry but it has to be even better to have a boat of your own. There must be a thousand secluded little bays to choose from around those islands.'

'There are. And I've got a mate at work—Dan, who's one of our anaesthetists, and he likes fishing as much as I do. It's not flash inside *Lassie*, but there's enough room for us to sleep in her and we can get started at the crack of dawn. There's nothing that tastes as good as a fresh snapper fillet buttie for breakfast.'

'You've got a frying pan on board, then?'

'I do. And thanks for the reminder—I need to replenish some supplies in her galley, like the olive oil I use in the pan. If you fancy a bit of a walk down the hill, you could come to the marina with me and have a look at her. I could give you a quick tour of the hospital too, if you like. Unless you need to sleep for a while? I remember how much harder it is doing a long-haul trip in this direction than it is going back home.'

Grace shook her head. 'I've been told the best

cure for jetlag is to stay awake until it's bedtime in your new time zone. And I'm feeling good. The taxi driver showed me where the hospital is, but it would be really helpful to know where to go when I turn up for work tomorrow. I'd love to see the marina too. It's so pretty, even from this distance.'

Jock took advantage of the way Grace was staring out at the view to let his own gaze rest on *her*.

She really was the perfect English rose, wasn't she? With skin that looked like porcelain, golden hair that was glowing in this bright light and eyes that were the colour of a summer sky. Or, even better, the colour the sea was today, which would normally be an irresistible invitation to get on his boat and get out there on a day off—to bask in the kind of serenity that never failed to make him feel a level of happiness he'd spent his whole life trying to find.

Jock found he had to drag his gaze away from Grace. It was probably just as well that Jenni had read him the riot act about hitting on her best friend.

Not that she'd needed to spell it out quite that clearly. Jock would never try it on with someone he was going to be sharing a house with. He'd discovered long ago how awkward it could become working with women he'd dated, even after they'd happily accepted that hooking up with him was just a bit of fun.

'Do not lay a single finger on her,' Jenni had said. *'She hasn't even been on one date since she escaped a really awful marriage and that was five years ago. She might look tough, Jock, but...she needs looking after, okay? Be the kind of brother you always were for me...'*

He might be on the opposite side of the globe but nothing would ever break the bond Jock had with his twin sister. Or how protective he'd always been of her. Looking out for her best friend was like an echo of the way he'd looked out for Jenni during the kind of childhood he wouldn't wish on anyone. It was a form of love and it required complete trust—on both sides. Trust that needed to be built, starting now.

So, no... Grace Collins had nothing to worry about as far as he was concerned. Disappointing Jenni was the last thing he'd want to do.

Jock got to his feet and held his hand out for Grace's empty plate. 'I'll look after that. Why don't you find some comfortable walking shoes and we'll head off?'

The small town had a rather delightful holiday destination feel to it.

Relaxed-looking people wearing sunhats and shorts were drinking coffee at outdoor cafés or browsing in shops. There were grassy areas with children's playgrounds, a caravan selling ice creams, seagulls drifting overhead and private boats of all shapes and sizes bobbing gently against their moorings at the marina.

'Half the fun of owning a boat is pottering around on days like this, doing stuff that needs doing,' Jock told Grace.

'I can see that.' Grace shook her head at the hand Jock was holding out to help her onto the boat. 'I'm good, thanks. Oh…' She looked around as she climbed on board. 'This is lovely…'

The boat was obviously well cared for and its wooden ship's wheel, panelling and brass fittings were gleaming. Jock opened cupboards to stow the canned food and other supplies he'd brought with him and showed Grace how neatly all the cooking utensils and other necessities were tucked into tiny spaces around the sink and cooktop. In the low space that was at the front of the boat were cushioned benches with more storage space. Rays of sunlight came in through small portholes.

'Is that a first aid kit?'

'Yes. Not that I can leave any drugs out here, but I'd hate to not have the basics if I find someone in trouble in some isolated spot.'

'Me too. I used to be a paramedic before I became a midwife.'

'Really? I didn't know that. What made you change direction?'

'I got sent to my first case of a woman in labour,' she said simply. 'She ended up giving birth in the back of the ambulance on the way to hospital and... I guess I fell in love with catching babies.'

It had been a call-out that had changed her entire life, not just her career. An experience that had given Grace a strength she'd never known she had and a way forward from the life she had thought she was trapped in for ever.

'It's magic, isn't it?' There was a soft smile in Jock's voice. 'When you hear that first cry and see them looking at the world for the very first time.'

'Mmm.' For Grace, it was the moment the mother got to hold her safely delivered baby in her arms. To feel that wash of relief that was always mixed in with the wonder of new life. Because it never, ever went away completely, did it? Knowing what it was like to have held her own baby, who had never had the chance to take her first breath...

This cabin space suddenly felt too closed in and she turned away to step out into the sunshine again. She saw a small dinghy heading towards the end of the marina. A man threw a rope around a bollard and jumped out onto the pier.

'What's going on?' Jock came out as the man

came rapidly towards them. 'Hey…mate? You okay?'

'Have you got a phone? My battery's dead and I need to call an ambulance.'

'I'm a doctor. What's happened? Has someone had an accident?'

The man shook his head. 'It's my wife. I can't get her out of the boat and I think the baby's coming…'

Jock's startled gaze caught Grace's. 'Could you grab that first aid kit?'

As Grace ducked back into the cabin to get the kit, she could hear him telling the man he'd come past the right boat because he was an obstetrician and had a midwife with him. He had already made a phone call by the time she came out again.

'Ambulance is on its way,' Jock said. He took the kit from Grace but opened a side pocket to give her some gloves to shove in her pocket. 'But I think we should go and see what's happening before it gets here.'

'*Please*…' the man begged. 'And I need to get back to Suzie. We're moored to an anchor buoy further out. My name's Oliver, by the way.'

Jock introduced himself and Grace as they followed Oliver.

'When's the baby due?' Grace asked.

'Not for another couple of weeks. We thought we could get one last weekend in. We came over from Nelson yesterday and we were going to go out for a nice lunch and then head back home this afternoon.' He was leading the way at a jog. 'We got told that first babies are usually late. And there's always lots of warning that labour's really started, isn't there?'

'Not always,' Grace said.

Jock was right behind her as she reached the ladder close to the dinghy. 'Any problems with Suzie's pregnancy?'

'No. Maybe because it's been so easy we thought we had this bit under control as well.' Oliver started the outboard motor. 'Suzie thought she'd just wet her pants but then the pains started and there was no way she could climb down to the dinghy.' He looked over his shoulder. 'I'll have to go back to get the ambulance crew, yeah?'

'They'll need to come out on a boat that can cope with a stretcher if it's needed. Don't worry— the coastguard headquarters is just down the road from the marina and they'll be able to sort out the logistics as soon as I can update them on the situation.' Jock was shading his eyes against the sun as they sped out to where boats were moored in open water. 'Our job is to get to Suzie and give her whatever support she needs.'

Grace took another glance at Jock's profile. How different was this version of her new colleague to the laidback, charming playboy she'd met only a few hours ago. This was Jock McKay the surgeon she was seeing now. Focused.

In charge.

This might be the last thing Grace could have expected as her first clinical experience in her new job but she couldn't be in better company, could she?

Her heart sank, however, as they got close to the sleek yacht that belonged to Oliver and Suzie. They could all hear the agonised cry coming from within the cabin.

'*Ollie*...where are you? I can't *do* this...'

Oliver looked as white as a ghost. He cut the motor but then looked as if he had no idea what he should do next. Jock stood up to steady the dinghy against the back of the yacht. 'You okay to climb up?' he asked Grace. 'It might be best if you go in first. I'll have a wee chat with Oliver and bring the kit in just a sec.'

A flash of a glance told Grace that he would prefer that Suzie didn't see her husband looking quite this terrified and she sent back a nod that was agreeing with more than her going in first. If this labour was already advanced enough to make it impossible to move the mother, hopefully, it would only be the skills of a midwife that would be needed. And if Oliver could be reassured enough to find the strength to support his wife, it could make a huge difference for everybody involved.

The interior cabin of a small yacht was not the ideal space for any kind of medical intervention. The ceiling was too low to be able to stand up straight and the gap between the cushioned bench seats that doubled as beds was barely enough at the pointy end for a person to turn around, let alone to set out any gear that might be needed.

Grace didn't seem perturbed, though, and Jock realised that her previous experience as a paramedic had to be a huge bonus. She was used to facing any kind of challenge in every kind of environment. She had her ponytail looped up into its fastening to keep her hair completely out of the way and her face was still enough to suggest utter concentration as she was giving Suzie an internal examination. Oliver had squeezed onto the cushion on the other side of the boat and was holding his wife's hand. They both had their heads on the widest part of the cushion in the bow.

Grace looked up at Jock.

'So the baby is in a longitudinal lie with a cephalic presentation. Suzie's fully dilated and in second stage of labour. She's not feeling the urge to push yet but I can feel baby's head. Foetal station one, possibly two...'

Jock nodded. A foetal station of one to two meant that the baby's head was already well into the birth canal. It also meant they wouldn't be moving Suzie.

'Oliver, could you find as many clean towels as you can?'

'Why?'

'I think your baby's pretty keen to get born on a boat.'

Oliver gulped and then wriggled backwards to go hunting for linen.

'You don't have a portable Doppler or a feto-scope in that kit of yours, do you, Jock?' Grace was pulling off her gloves and reaching for a clean pair. 'It would be good to get a heart rate.'

'No.' And Jock knew that what was even more important was to be able to detect changes in the heart rate, which could be a warning that the baby was in distress. 'But I do have a stethoscope.' He pulled open the zip on the kit.

'*Oh...*' Suzie groaned loudly.

'Another contraction?' Grace asked. She checked her watch. 'That's only two minutes since the last one finished.'

'I need to push...' Suzie sounded like she was speaking through gritted teeth. 'Oh... *God... No...*'

'You're doing great,' Oliver told her. 'Remember to breathe...'

Suzie swore at him.

Jock had the stethoscope in his ears. He had to squeeze against Grace to get close enough to put the disc of the stethoscope against the stretched skin of Suzie's abdomen that felt as solid as concrete right now. The contraction made it harder to locate the best position to hear the baby's heart and Suzie's cries made it difficult to hear anything at all.

'I feel sick,' she said between loud groans. 'I need to go to the loo… Oh…it *hurts*…'

'Save your breath for pushing,' Oliver suggested.

Suzie swore at him again.

'Heart rate's one thirty,' Jock told Grace. Normal. They shared a glance that was relieved.

And Grace's calm voice had an ability to cut through the rising tension. 'You're doing so well, Suzie. I can see baby's head now… He's going to be here very soon…'

Jock could see the baby's head appearing as well.

And then it went backwards far enough for the chin to vanish in what appeared to be a classic 'turtle sign' that was an indication of the baby's shoulders being stuck.

A warning of a potential obstetric emergency.

This time, the glance he shared with Grace was

intense but Jock kept his voice as calm as hers had been.

'Swap places?'

It was awkward because there was not enough space for two people to pass without considerable body contact, but again Grace managed to make it seem easy. Perhaps that was because she was just as focused on their patient as he was.

'Suzie…? We're going to put you in a different position to see if we can make your next contraction more effective, okay?' Jock was about to ask Grace to help move Suzie to abduct and hyperflex her thighs onto her abdomen but she was already moving.

'McRobert's?' she murmured.

'Yes. Thanks… Okay, Suzie, we're going to shift your position to make a bit more room to help things along.'

The wall of the boat made it trickier for Jock to get one leg into position but Grace was ahead of him on the other side, lifting and squeezing the leg into the position that could rotate her pelvis and widen the opening to release the baby's shoulder.

'I can't do this,' Suzie wailed. 'It hurts…'

'What's going on?' Oliver demanded. 'Why are you doing that?'

Suzie was beginning her next contraction and Jock found he was holding his breath. He'd taken note of the time when the baby's head had first appeared and the countdown was on to deliver this baby. They only had a few minutes before they could run into real trouble.

'Sometimes the baby can get a bit stuck for a moment,' Grace told him. 'This is the best way to get past that.'

'You could help hold Suzie's legs, Oliver,' Jock suggested.

'Climb past me on the other side and get near her head,' Grace added.

Suzie's cry of pain was sharp. Oliver scrambled to get to her.

'Hold your legs behind your knees,' Grace instructed Suzie as she leaned back against her husband. 'Oliver can put his hands over yours and help you pull your legs as close as possible to your chest. And don't push, Suzie... Just blow...' Grace was demonstrating the breathing to remind Suzie how to help quell the urge to push.

'Grace? Can you give me some suprapubic pressure, please?'

Jock was pleased to see her locate where the anterior shoulder of the baby was and then link her hands in a CPR position directly behind the shoulder and apply pressure in a rocking motion. She knew exactly what she was doing, didn't she? Jock could let himself think ahead in case this technique wasn't successful.

He had a scalpel in his kit so he could perform an episiotomy to make it easier to perform the internal manoeuvres of slipping his hand in to get hold of the posterior arm and get this baby out. The clock was ticking. The tension was increasing rapidly.

The whole boat started rocking as more people climbed on board. There was no hope of any extra rescuers fitting into this cabin space, but they didn't need to.

'I can feel baby moving…' Grace said. 'I think we're almost there, Suzie…'

And, just as suddenly as it had begun, the potential emergency evaporated as the baby slithered out into Jock's hands.

Even better, this baby boy, who was big enough that his size had probably caused the worrying hiccup in his arrival, began crying instantly and, in this confined space under the deck of the boat, the sound was so loud it made his parents laugh.

And then cry.

It looked like Grace had tears in her own eyes.

'Apgar at one minute is eight,' Jock announced.

'Is that good?' Oliver asked.

'It's great,' Grace assured them. 'Let's get baby onto Mum's skin to keep him warm. Do you want to cut the cord in a minute when we're ready, Dad?'

Oliver sounded a lot more confident now. 'Absolutely.'

Grace hesitated before picking the baby up, however, because she could see what Jock was checking as he carefully felt around the baby's shoulders.

'All good,' he said quietly. 'No fractures of either clavicle.'

Yes…they were tears, but she was smiling. Not at him, but at the baby she gathered into her hands to transfer him to his mother's skin. He could see the joy in her face and he could sense the extraordinary satisfaction she got from her profession.

He could *feel* her passion.

Jock loved meeting people who felt the same way he did about the job he'd chosen to devote his life to. He appreciated working with people who were intelligent and capable and exceptionally good at what they did.

And, okay…he couldn't deny that he liked being around very beautiful women.

Like the one who seemed to be waiting to catch his gaze as she rested her hand on Suzie's abdomen.

Suzie was so entranced with her baby she didn't seem to be noticing the new contraction she was experiencing, but Jock shifted his attention to the last stage of labour and the delivery of the placenta.

Most of his attention, anyway.

A part of his brain was still collating all the

positive attributes he was discovering about his new colleague, who was also—at least for the moment—his new flatmate.

Grace Collins might be out of bounds, but she was, quite possibly, his perfect woman.

No...on second thoughts, maybe the fact that she was out of bounds was exactly *why* she was his perfect woman.

No matter how attractive she was, if Jock even thought of responding to that he would see his sister in the back of his mind, wagging her finger at him, and that would be more than enough to remind him to back off. On the other side of that coin, however, that meant he wouldn't have to walk away as soon as an uncomfortable level of closeness was reached.

He could follow Jenni's edict and look after her like a big brother. Which meant he could have fun with Grace. Tease her like he would tease Jenni. Enjoy a conversation or going out somewhere together without being on alert for any hidden agenda.

Aye...this was as safe as it got.

And that made it perfect.

CHAPTER TWO

WAKING UP THE next morning, Grace had a very disconcerting few seconds wondering, quite literally, where on earth she was.

And then she heard the faint sound of someone whistling.

A male person whistling, and that was far more disconcerting than not knowing where she was.

Grace froze in her new bed, looking up at a high ceiling with an ornate plaster centrepiece that the light was dangling from. The plaster flowers were creating shadows because there was sunlight filtering through curtains that she hadn't pulled shut properly last night, when jet-lag had rendered her incoherent enough to crash into unconsciousness by seven p.m.

Remembering where she was made her suck in a huge breath.

The reality of being alone in a house with a male person made that breath catch in her chest. Had she really thought she would be okay with this?

She found herself letting that breath out slowly enough for it to be soothing. Reassuring.

That was Jock McKay whistling.

Her best friend's brother.

The man with the twinkle in his eyes and the cheeky grin, who couldn't have made her feel more welcome when she'd arrived yesterday. Good grief...his first words had been to offer her something to eat, as if he'd just been waiting for the opportunity to look after her. How could she possibly feel nervous about being in this house with a man like that?

This was a man who'd looked positively misty when he'd told her that he thought there was magic involved in bringing babies into the world, but had then demonstrated his scientific skill and absolute focus by doing exactly that.

Above all, he was Jenni's brother and she'd told her that she'd be as safe as houses.

And wasn't being able to take a huge leap of faith underpinning everything about this enormous change she was making in her life?

That didn't stop the nerves kicking in, of course, as Grace threw her clothes on before heading for the bathroom and then the kitchen, where she found Jock rinsing some dishes.

'Morning, Sleeping Beauty,' he said. 'How did you sleep?'

'Like the dead,' Grace told him. 'I'm not sure

I'm quite awake yet, to be honest. It feels like I'm still dreaming.'

There was that grin again. And the gleam of warmth that made his eyes the most remarkable shade of blue. Grace felt herself releasing another slow breath.

This was okay. She *could* cope.

'You need coffee,' Jock told her. 'I'd offer to make it, but I need to see all my patients before my Theatre list starts at eight.'

'You don't need to look after me, Jock.'

'Oh, I think I do. Jenni will have my guts for garters if I don't.'

Grace laughed. 'I'm more than capable of making my own coffee.'

'There's plenty of bread for toast. You'll find jam and Vegemite in the same cupboard as the coffee.'

'Vegemite?'

'Like Marmite, but not nearly as intense. I love it.' Jock was heading out of the kitchen. 'You're coming into the hospital today?'

'Yes. I'm getting the grand tour and induction process so I'll be ready to hit the ground running when I officially start on Wednesday.'

'Might see you round. If you want to go exploring later, you're welcome to use my car. The keys are on my bedside table.'

'Thank you. But I won't need a car.'

One of Jock's eyebrows rose. 'You do drive, don't you?'

'Of course I do. I used to drive an ambulance, remember? But the hospital's an easy walk from here.'

'Yes, but your home visits won't be. They could be an hour or more's drive away. You might want to start getting to know the roads.'

'I think I get to use a hospital car for home visits, but you're right—I will need to get a car of my own soon so I can get out and see as much of New Zealand as possible.'

'Now, that's something I *could* help you with. I know a guy at one of the local car yards. Best I come with you, though, and make sure you get the best price.'

'What time is it for you?'

'Just coming up to five p.m. What about you?' Jenni seemed to be peering into her phone screen. 'Looks like you're having breakfast. Ooh…what's that black stuff on your toast? Marmite?'

'Vegemite. My new fave. With toasted wholegrain bread. You let it get a bit cold and put lots of butter on first. I hear it's even better with some avocado on top, but I haven't tried that yet.'

'Yuck…'

Grace ignored the face Jenni was making. 'And it's six a.m. here. It's going to be a glorious day.

Look at that…' She turned her phone around. 'Can you see how blue that sky is already?'

'I don't want to know,' Jenni grumbled. 'It's been snowing here again today. Well…sleeting, which means that there's slush everywhere. And it's *freezing*…'

'Tell me more.' Grace was grinning as she reached for her mug of coffee.

'No. You're too happy as it is. I'm dead jealous.'

'Have you booked some tickets to come and visit yet?'

'Working on it. It's not cheap travelling that far. And Fergus wants me to go to Portugal with him for a weekend.'

'Isn't Fergus the guy you hooked up with before I left Glasgow?'

'That's the one.'

Grace laughed. 'I wouldn't book Portugal then.'

'Why not?'

'It's been nearly three weeks. You'll be breaking your own record if it lasts longer than a month.'

'That's a bit harsh.'

'You're as bad as Jock. He's got a bit of a reputation of being a playboy here, although nobody seems to think any less of him for it. He's a popular lad, your brother.'

'That's why it's good to keep things casual. If it's clear it's never going to get serious, nobody's going to get hurt and you can just enjoy it.'

Grace used taking a bite of toast as a reason to avoid having to respond to that statement. Maybe she was out of sync with the majority of her generation but casual sex had never appealed to her.

And now…well, it was the stuff of nightmares, wasn't it?

'But you're right,' Jenni added. 'I won't book Portugal. I'll put the money towards that ticket to New Zealand instead. If that's a deal breaker for Fergus, so be it. What are you up to today?'

'I've got an almost forty-two weeker who's coming in for an induction first thing, so she could well deliver later today. And then I've got an antenatal clinic this afternoon. If it's anything like almost every shift I've had here so far it'll be full-on, but at least I'm starting to get used to where everything is now and I can find my way around. That nervousness and how tiring it is to be the new girl at school is finally wearing off.'

'But you're loving this job, aren't you?'

'Yeah…' Grace glanced at her watch. 'Speaking of which, I'd better go and get myself ready. I can't keep sitting here and looking at all the boats in the harbour and the sunshine glistening on the sea. Did I tell you that Jock said I could come out on his boat next time he and his friend Dan go fishing? If I'm lucky, I might be able to go swimming with some dolphins.'

'Oh, *stop*…' But Jenni was laughing. 'Is he

around? I could annoy him for a wee while until Fergus gets here to take me out on the town.'

'No…he's out for a run. Or was it a game of squash? I can't keep up with his fitness regime. Maybe it's a bit like his love life. Endless variety and always something on the go.'

Jenni laughed. 'You haven't come across any more semi-naked women in the house, have you?'

'No. I think he's gone underground while I'm settling in. There has been a night or two when he's been very late home.' Grace picked up the last corner of her toast as she got to her feet.

'Is it as bad as you thought it would be, having to live with a guy? Are you still planning to find a place of your own?'

Grace gestured that she couldn't say anything because her mouth was full, but that gave her a moment to consider her friend's question and, to her surprise, she realised she'd almost forgotten that had been her original plan. That, even on a temporary basis, the idea of living with a man— if he hadn't been Jenni's brother—could easily have been a dealbreaker for coming here in the first place at all.

Maybe that tension had been defused by the fact that Greta had been here when she'd first arrived. Or that Jock had been so laid back and welcoming, with that 'it's no big deal' and 'the more the merrier' kind of vibe that had somehow sneaked past her defences—possibly due to being dazed by jetlag.

Or maybe it had been that totally unexpected introduction to working with one of her new colleagues when they'd delivered that baby in the bottom of that yacht. It could have been the jokes on the way home about the water birth where nobody had even got wet because, later that evening, before she'd crashed into the deepest sleep ever, Grace realised that Jock was the first man who had made her laugh since…well…since her life had slipped towards the cliff she had inevitably fallen over.

But it was more likely to have been the way she'd felt working with Jock like that, being thrown into the deep end and having nothing to rely on other than each other. The focus that felt like she was looking into a professional mirror. The need for the arrival of a new life to be, above all, *safe*…

That was it, in a nutshell.

It wasn't just because the rent was subsidised in this hospital-provided accommodation. Grace was letting go of the idea of moving out because *she* felt safe.

And why would she want to fix something if it wasn't broken?

Okay, there had been the odd moment in the first few days when she'd frozen, like she had when she'd woken up that first day, wondering where on earth she was. It had happened again a day or two later, when she'd come out of her room to see Jock emerging from the bathroom with only a towel around his waist and she'd been hit with a curl of sensation in her gut that took her breath away. And the time she'd been in the kitchen and heard the click of the front door opening as he'd arrived home and she'd felt a familiar chill trickle down her spine.

But, now on her way to the same kitchen as she swallowed her last mouthful of breakfast, Grace had the distinct feeling she wasn't ever going to overreact like that again. It felt like she was moving on in bigger ways than changing her location and lifestyle so convincingly.

'He's been brilliant,' she told Jenni. 'He got me such a good deal on the car I bought last week. He came with me for a test drive and then drove the hardest bargain with the car salesman.'

And that had been a test for something more than how the car handled, hadn't it? She'd been beside Jock in a small hatchback car. Close enough that it would have been so easy for him to touch her and…she'd still felt safe.

She'd seen the envious look the receptionist in the car yard had given her when she was signing the sales agreement for the little blue car—the one that told her how lucky she was that she had a super cute boyfriend to help her buy a car and, if she was honest, Grace had rather liked the assumption being made.

Not that she would ever confess that to Jenni.

'He's a really good cook,' she added hurriedly. 'He makes the best bacon butties in the world and sometimes he even remembers to put the loo seat down.'

Grace tried not to let her smile stretch too far across her face. She didn't want to make Jenni feel bad that she was settling in so easily to her new life. That she felt so much safer than she had, thanks to living so far away from the UK—and her past. That she was feeling happier than she had in…possibly for ever?

'I always wanted a brother when I was growing up and now it feels like I've got one,' she finished with genuine sincerity. 'And he looks so much like you that it helps me to not miss you so much.'

'Aww…' Jenni made a sad face. 'Now I feel really left out. And I'm missing *you* heaps. Say hi to Jock for me.'

The first time Grace saw Jock at work later that morning certainly wasn't the time to pass on any greeting from his sister.

Her patient, Melissa, who had gone well past her estimated date of delivery with her first child, had been scheduled to have an induction this morning but had, instead, come into hospital in active labour and four centimetres dilated at almost the same time Grace had arrived to start her shift. Her birth plan included an epidural for pain relief and it was Jock's fishing buddy, Dan, who arrived to give Melissa the spinal anaesthetic. A tall, serious man, he said very little after asking for current vital signs for the mother and whether the foetal monitoring was giving any cause for concern. Grace helped him position Melissa, sitting on the edge of the bed with her spine curved, and supported her shoulders as Dan did his work swiftly and efficiently, inserting a fine catheter to allow release of medication that could be topped up as needed by the patient-controlled button on the infusion.

Hours later, however, the contractions were slowing down, her dilation hadn't progressed at all, Melissa's anxiety was increasing and, even more concerning, the baby was beginning to show signs of being distressed, with the heart rate slowing during contractions and then taking a little longer each time to go back up. When Melissa's waters broke and there were signs of meconium in the fluid, Grace paged Jock, as the obstetrician on call, to come down to the labour suite, where she introduced him to Melissa and her partner Jason.

'Mel's a thirty-four-year-old primigravida,' she added. 'No complications with the pregnancy but she's at forty-one weeks, five days from her EDD, and was due to have an induction this morning because of reduced foetal movements yesterday.'

'Hey, Mel.' Jock was wearing pale blue scrubs and had a stethoscope slung around his neck. He was quickly scanning the patient's notes as Grace was speaking and would have noted both the presence of meconium in the amniotic fluid and the decelerations of the baby's heart rate during contractions, but his smile as he looked up at Melissa was more than reassuring. He looked impressed, even.

'I see you decided to jump the gun and go into labour all by yourself this morning,' he said. 'Good for you, getting a head start like that.'

It was the first time Grace had seen Melissa smile since she'd arrived that morning and she could understand why. She'd feel reassured herself if Jock was standing beside her bed, looking as if he was proud of the effort she was making to have her baby and that he was ready to help her in any way she needed. As if nothing was a problem and the only person that mattered in this moment was the person he was focused on. For an exhausted, frightened first-time mother—and her husband, who was hovering nervously beside her—he was the medical equivalent of a knight in shining armour.

He represented hope that the worst was over.

And he brought a new level of safety to an increasingly tense situation. Grace could see both Melissa and Jason almost breathing a sigh of relief. It wasn't that they didn't have faith in their midwife, it was more that they were being reminded that they were in the right place, with the best people and resources they could have around them.

And who wouldn't trust Jock McKay?

That quintessential boy-next-door friendliness and dependability was so obviously genuine. Melissa and her partner couldn't know the level of professional competence that Jock possessed but perhaps they could sense the respect with which other staff members regarded him. They would certainly be able to feel that he was more than interested in his patients—that he cared about both his mothers and their babies. As deeply as Grace cared about each and every mother she worked with to help bring their babies safely into the world.

She really liked that about him.

His examination of Melissa was gentle but thorough. He watched her go into another contraction and they could all hear the ominous dip in the baby's heart rate on the CTG machine that was monitoring her through the flat discs strapped to her abdomen. A new section of graph paper began emerging as part of the automatic recording when acceptable parameters were being breached. Grace had silenced the alarms to prevent the additional anxiety they would cause.

Jock perched his hip on the edge of the bed, which made his eye level much closer to Melissa's as she took a bunch of tissues from her husband and wiped tears from her face. Grace was on the other side of the bed and took hold of the hand Melissa stretched out towards her.

'You're doing a great job,' Jock told her quietly. 'But it's been a wee bit too long without any progress and I think your baby's getting tired too. The safest option for both of you would be for you to have a Caesarean section.'

Melissa nodded. Grace had already discussed this possibility with them. 'I just want this to be over,' she said. 'To have her out so that we know she's okay…'

'Which is exactly what we want too,' Jock said. 'Grace is going to get you ready and I'll see you up in Theatre. You've already got an epidural so you're good to go. And you've met Dan, our anaesthetist on duty today. He'll be in Theatre with us too, to help look after you.' His smile included Jason now. 'You guys will be meeting your baby very soon. Have you got any questions you'd like to ask?'

Melissa stifled a sob. 'Is Jason allowed to be there the whole time?'

'Of course. Grace, are you okay to organise the theatre gear for Jason?'

'Yes. I'll find everything he needs.'

'You'll be right beside Melissa at the head of the bed,' Jock told Jason. 'You won't be able to see the actual surgery because we put a screen up, but you'll be able to talk to her and hold her hand. Dan will be able to answer any questions you might have.'

'But Grace will be there too?'

'She's your midwife.' Jock's smile was for Grace this time. 'I might be doing the actual delivery this time but I'm quite sure she wouldn't want to be anywhere else.'

'He's not wrong,' Grace said. 'We're all going to be there to take the very best care of you and baby, Mel.'

Jock *hadn't* been wrong. Grace had always enjoyed every part of being in the surgical team performing a Caesarean section. She loved being in Theatre during the preparation, where her job was to check that the resuscitation unit was turned on to pre-warm and the settings were correct for delivering the suction and oxygen functions. She loved getting both herself and the father-to-be ready to enter Theatre with the clothing and hats, masks and shoe covers, along with plenty of encouragement and reassurance for what was a frightening prospect for someone who hadn't expected to end up being rushed into an operating theatre.

She loved waiting to one side of the sterile area as the surgeon and their assistants worked, ready to receive the baby in a sterile towel—as long as the delivery was uncomplicated—show the infant to the parents and then take it to the warming unit to do the initial examination. Because this surgical delivery was happening urgently due to foetal distress, there would be a paediatrician standing by for possible resuscitation but, for the moment, Grace could stand alone and watch the first minutes of the operation.

She could watch Jock engaged in one of the most dramatic ways to help bring a baby into the world and she held her breath as she saw him start a procedure she'd observed countless times, but it was always a little bit different.

The steps were familiar. The horizontal incision low on the abdomen that exposed the layer of fat, followed by muscle and then the gleaming globe of the uterus. The smell of blood vessels being cauterised and the sound of the suction unit clearing amniotic fluid were also familiar enough to be welcomed and Grace wasn't surprised by the frown of concentration she could see on Jock's face as he reached in to free the baby, who was probably well engaged in the pelvis after the hours of Melissa's labour.

'I can feel something...' Melissa's cry was alarmed.

'You should be able to feel pressure.' Jock's voice was calm. 'But it shouldn't hurt.'

'It's not hurting, is it?' The anaesthetist, Dan, leaned forward so that Melissa could see his face.

'No...it just feels...weird...'

'Not long now. Hang in there,' Jock said.

The baby's head was out and the theatre nurse quickly suctioned the tiny nose and mouth. Grace stepped closer, a sterile towel in her gloved hands, as Jock wriggled the shoulders free.

'And here we are...' He held the baby up between both hands, with a secure grip under her arms and supporting her head, high enough to be seen by the parents over the drape that was clipped to a frame to provide a screen. The tiny legs were still curled up and the rope of the umbilical cord hung beneath her.

'She's gorgeous,' he pronounced.

Then, before the cord was clamped and cut, Jock turned his head to look at the baby himself, holding her in front of his own face—for just a heartbeat—as if he was making eye contact to reassure himself that everything was all right. The baby's eyes were open and she seemed to be looking right back at him, too startled to move.

And there it was again.

That moment that never quite went away for Grace.

The echo of that awful silence when you just knew that everything wasn't okay. That it would never be okay ever again. When your future—and the world as you knew it—had just been derailed into complete catastrophe.

The memory was no more than a ghost. So fleeting it almost wasn't there these days, but it was what happened next that was almost Grace's undoing on this occasion.

Jock smiled at the baby.

Grace couldn't see his mouth under his mask but she could see the way his eyes crinkled and his body language softened in a glow that was like a telepathic welcome to this new little human.

It felt a lot like love and that gave Grace a squeeze on her heart that was so painful it almost made her gasp. Jock would probably smile at his own baby like that as it took its first breath, wouldn't he?

The way she had once, for a nanosecond, after her baby was born. Before she'd remembered what the silence around her meant. That there wasn't going to be a first breath...

The ghost evaporated in the same moment that she remembered something that Jenni had said that day the direction of her life had begun to change—that the only long-term commitment Jock McKay was ever going to make would be to the boat he'd fallen in love with and purchased. It was unlikely he would ever be having telepathic conversations in his own baby's first moments of life but, oddly, that only made it feel as if there was more of a bond between herself and Jock.

The baby didn't seem too impressed by Jock's attention. She scrunched up her little face and was crying vigorously as she got her umbilical cord clamped and cut and was then laid onto the towel Grace had over her hands. She could take her to the parents for a closer, brief peek before the first, more thorough assessment of the tiny girl's condition was done in the warmth of the resuscitation unit.

Given the all-clear from the paediatrician, Grace could then swaddle the baby in towels to keep her warm and put her into her father's arms as he sat beside Melissa while the longer part of the surgery happened, with the removal of the placenta and the painstaking closure of all the layers of the abdomen.

And that gave Grace another chance to watch Jock.

To remember that conversation with Jenni early this morning that had made her realise how happy she was that she'd made the decision to leave her old life behind. Because it really did feel as if it was a long way behind her now.

It almost felt as if the brush of that ghost, when she'd seen Jock holding Melissa's baby girl in the air to make eye contact with the newborn, might have been the last time it was going to hurt quite that much.

Grace didn't realise that her lips had curved into a hint of a smile that must have shown in her eyes until she turned back to Melissa and caught a glance from Dan on the way.

Oh, help…did he think she was smiling at *him*?

Her heart skipped a beat and sped up, and not in the good way of being attracted to someone— it was more like a faint touch of panic. That embryonic smile evaporated instantly.

Grace wasn't trying to attract the attention of any man. She had, in fact, perfected more than one or two techniques to make sure she *didn't*.

Clearly, there were still some parts of her past that weren't far enough behind her yet.

Maybe they never would be.

As if he sensed something untoward, Jock lifted his head from his stitching to glance at Grace.

Just a glance, nothing more. But it was enough.

Whatever was threatening her peace of mind and joy in this particular moment was gone. It felt like Grace's feet were back on solid ground.

Yeah… Jock was here and…it felt safe again.

CHAPTER THREE

'STELLA WATSON?'

The woman who was sitting quietly in the corner of the outpatient department waiting room, staring out of the window, jumped visibly as Grace called her name.

'I'm so sorry to have kept you waiting for so long, Stella. Antenatal clinics can get a bit hectic. I'm Grace, one of the midwives here. Come with me...'

Hectic was the word for it today, that was for sure. The departmental staff had been very helpful but this was the first antenatal clinic Grace had run by herself in what was not simply a new work environment but a new country with slightly different protocols, and she was still familiarising herself with what was offered during pregnancy in the way of appointment schedules, tests, vaccinations and birthing options.

Fortunately, the basics of the monitoring that needed to be done at all stages of a woman's countdown to giving birth were familiar enough to be automatic and Grace had been busy all afternoon meeting her patients, taking blood pressures and doing urine dipstick analyses and physical examinations to check the position of the baby and fundal height and listening to heart sounds. She'd booked ultrasound scans, ordered blood tests, discussed any symptoms or worries, offered advice and made plans for any follow-up needed before the next scheduled visit. She'd picked up toys thrown around her consulting room by preschoolers who had accompanied their mothers and recorded every measurement, along with scribbling copious notes so that she could complete her paperwork later and not keep people waiting too long as appointment slots invariably ran over time and it was frustrating not to have had more time to get to know these women she was meeting for the first time.

Like Maureen Petersen, a forty-year-old primigravida who had just passed the halfway point of her pregnancy and was carrying a recent ultrasound image of her baby in her wallet. She took that out to show Grace as she got up to leave an appointment where every check had been reassuringly normal.

'I keep looking at it,' she'd confided in Grace. 'Because it seems too good to be true. My friends think I'm crazy to choose to become a single mother at my age but…it felt like my last chance, you know? And I thought, why should I have to miss out on being a mum just because I haven't found a partner? I know it won't be easy but I'm not scared to do it by myself. Except for the birth bit… I am a bit scared of that.'

'You won't be doing that by yourself,' Grace promised. 'We'll be taking care of you through the rest of your pregnancy and the birth, and for the first six weeks of you being at home with your baby.'

'Will it be you there for the birth?'

'That might depend on whether baby wants to play ball,' Grace said. 'But I really hope so. And I'll be looking forward to seeing you at your next appointment. In the meantime, call any time if you're worried about anything.'

At least the pressure was off for the last appointment for this clinic. Stella Watson had been put at the end of the list because this was a first antenatal visit and would need more time, especially when the patient file was empty apart from a GP's very brief referral form. Grace needed to know about any significant health issues and current medications or allergies and past medical history for both the mother-to-be and her family. She would also be gathering any impression that extra care might be needed due to any individual physical, social or emotional needs.

Grace shifted the chairs so that they were both on the same side of the desk.

'So I understand that this is your second pregnancy, Stella?'

'Yes.'

'How old is your first child?'

'He's…six.'

Grace made a quick note. There could be all sorts of reasons for a longer than normal gap between children. Commonly, it was as simple as a relationship break-up and a new baby with a new partner. It could be due to fertility issues and it might be the result of Stella losing a child before or after birth. It was definitely a subject that Grace needed to approach with sensitivity.

'And you didn't have your first baby here?'

'No, I was living up north. We only moved here recently. My husband got a job down on the wharf.'

Stella glanced over her shoulder as if she half-expected someone to come into the room. Or was she looking for a way out?

Something didn't feel right.

'Are you okay for childcare today?' Grace checked. 'You're not in a rush to get back home to…what's your son's name?'

'Scott. No, it's okay—I'm not in a hurry.'

Grace wasn't convinced. She glanced again

at the referral note to request the antenatal appointment.

'So you're not sure when your last period was?'

Stella shook her head. 'There's been a lot going on, what with finding a new place to live and shifting and getting Scott started at his new school and everything.'

'I totally get it,' Grace sympathised. 'I've only moved to Picton very recently myself. It's such a big upheaval in your life, isn't it? And it's not a problem.' She made another note. 'I might see if they can fit you in for a quick ultrasound, which will be able to give us an estimated date of delivery. What we'll do in the meantime is just have a chat so I can ask you about your medical history and your last pregnancy and so on. I'll take some baseline recordings like your blood pressure and weight. We'll do a blood and urine test, if that's okay, but today's appointment is mainly a chance for us to meet each other.' She made eye contact with Stella as she smiled warmly. 'I'm really looking forward to helping you in whatever way I can so you can really enjoy this pregnancy.'

Stella was staring at Grace, her eyes wide. 'But…but I don't *want* to enjoy this pregnancy,' she whispered. 'I don't want to be pregnant at all…' She burst into tears. '*Sorry*,' she sobbed. 'I'm really sorry…'

'You've got nothing to be sorry about…' Grace

leaned closer and put her hand over Stella's. 'It's okay,' she said. 'Talk to me...please?'

But Stella shook her head. She grabbed her bag from the floor beside her chair and stood up so fast she knocked her chair over as she turned. Before Grace could even say anything else, Stella had wrenched the door to the room open and she was gone.

Jock had no chance to avoid the woman, who walked straight into him as he came out of the coffee shop in the hospital foyer, probably because she was almost running. She had her head down, which meant she hadn't seen him.

And she was crying...

It was totally instinctive to catch the woman's shoulders and steady her, but Jock didn't let go straight away. It wasn't that it was unusual to see upset people coming and going in a hospital environment, when they could be visiting seriously ill family members or might have just lost a loved one. Perhaps this woman had been given bad news about her own health, given that she seemed to be running from the direction of the outpatient department.

'Hey...' Jock tried to catch her gaze. 'Is everything okay?'

Stupid question when it was clear that something was very wrong, but Jock could sense the panic this woman was experiencing and he needed to say something to let her know that he was there. That he was willing to help if he could.

'You might hurt yourself if you're not watching where you're going,' he added.

'Sorry… Oh, God…' She looked up, finally. 'Did I hurt *you*?'

'Not at all.' Jock smiled at her. 'Made of steel, I am.' He was about to let go of her shoulders as he felt her relax a little, but then he saw someone else coming out of the outpatient department's entrance.

And the concern on Grace's face as she approached them let him connect the dots instantly.

'I think someone might be looking for you,' he said.

'Stella?' Grace was close enough to call without attracting attention. 'Oh, thank goodness you're still here.' She lowered her voice even more. 'Please don't run away—we can talk about anything.'

Jock could feel how tense Stella was again. Something was very wrong and if she had run from an appointment with a midwife it was very likely that there was some kind of problem with a pregnancy.

'I was heading home,' he said casually, 'but I'm not in any hurry if there's anything I can help with.' It wasn't strictly true. Jock hadn't got near his boat in days and he had been planning to make the most of a long summer's evening and head out for a spot of fishing.

'Jock's one of our obstetricians,' Grace told Stella.

Stella pulled away from him as if his hands were burning her shoulders.

'I can't do it.' Her whisper was terrified. 'I can't have this baby.' She was turning towards the main entrance. 'I've got to get out of here.'

'No problem.' Jock caught Grace's startled look as he agreed with Stella. 'We can't make you stay. But could you do something for me first?'

Stella also looked startled. 'What?'

'At least talk to Grace. Please...even if it's only for a few minutes.'

'Why?'

'Because she's new here and it was her first an-tenatal clinic today and I don't think she's used to having one of her mums running away from her.'

'Oh...' Stella bit her lip. 'Sorry...'

'So you'll talk to her?'

Stella nodded slowly. 'Okay... I guess I owe her that much...'

Grace caught Jock's gaze and he could see her lips moving in a silent 'thank you' as she led Stella back into Outpatients.

It made him feel surprisingly good that he might have done something that Grace really appreciated. Jenni would be happy too. Jock could already imagine making a joke of it and telling his sister that he'd stopped one of her friend's patients escaping.

Except that it wasn't anything to joke about, was it?

And he'd inadvertently become involved in Stella's case. He wanted to know the story behind what had happened and what was going to happen next.

Jock gave up on his plan to go fishing. He'd go to the supermarket instead and find something to cook for Grace when she got home.

'That smells *so* good.' The aroma had been making Grace's stomach rumble, in fact, even before she'd walked through the gate of her new home.

'It's nothing fancy. I'm doing bangers and mash for dinner—just to make sure you don't start feeling homesick.'

'It smells a lot fancier than the bangers and mash I used to get at the local pub.' Grace dropped her bag and stepped closer to the small barbecue Jock was using at the end of the veranda.

'These ones are traditional British beef sausages, but they do come from a gourmet butcher in town and they do fancy snarlers too. Like wild venison and fennel. Or pork and parsley. I wasn't sure what you'd like so I played it safe.'

'Snarlers?'

'It's Kiwi for bangers. I believe it comes from the sound they make when they're trapped in a frying pan.'

Grace laughed. 'I like it. Can I do anything to help?'

'No. It's all good.'

Grace sank onto the chair with a sigh. 'Jenni says hi, by the way. I've been trying to find a moment to tell you that all day, but things kept happening.'

'They have a habit of doing that, don't they? When were you talking to Jenni?'

'This morning, while I was having breakfast.' Grace leaned her head back and closed her eyes. Had it only been this morning that she'd been sitting here eating her Vegemite toast? She blew out a breath. 'It's been quite a day.'

'It has,' Jock agreed. 'A great one for Melissa. It was a good call on your part, not leaving her in labour any longer.'

Grace liked that Jock remembered their patient's name and hadn't just referred to her as a case, like 'this morning's C-section'.

He was using tongs to turn the sausages on the grill as they got licked by flames. 'How did you get on with Stella after I left?' he asked.

'We talked for an hour or more. That's why I'm late. Poor thing, she's got... Oh, what's it called again? That extreme fear of pregnancy and labour?'

'Tokophobia.' Jock was nodding. 'Did you find any obvious cause?'

'Yes.' Grace sat up straighter. 'She had one of the more traumatic birth stories I've ever heard. Not from here,' she added hastily, as she saw Jock's shocked expression. 'It was in a small hospital up north somewhere. Six years ago.'

'What happened?'

'First pregnancy. Went into labour at forty weeks and seemed to be doing well but, twenty-three hours later, the baby was in distress. Two failed attempts with a vacuum cup, an episiotomy with inadequate analgesia and a forceps delivery that sounds like it was a struggle. There was probably a bit of shoulder dystocia going on as well.'

'Good grief…sounds like something out of the Middle Ages.'

'She's lucky her son survived. He had the cord wrapped around his neck as well. And, just to add insult to injury, they did a manual extraction of the placenta without waiting for an effective anaesthetic. Stella said that was the worst of the whole experience. The pain was unbelievable.'

Jock shook his head. 'No wonder she's terrified. What was the reason for such an urgent removal of the placenta? Did she have a post-partum haemorrhage?'

'I don't know. I've requested to have her hospital notes forwarded.'

'Good thinking. It might help if there are some medical explanations to what went on, even if they don't excuse the result. Has she talked to anyone about it?'

'I don't think she's ever talked about it. She thought it would be better to put it all behind her. She's done everything she can to avoid getting pregnant again, but her husband's desperate for another child so she thought she could force herself to go through it for his sake. She hasn't even told him she's pregnant though, because…' Grace had to take a breath to try and stop the wobble in her voice. 'She thinks she wants a termination—without him having to know anything about it.'

'What did *you* say?' The encouraging glance from Jock told Grace that he understood that it could have been distressing for her to hear that.

'I managed to get a dating scan done for her and she's only around eight to nine weeks along, so I said she didn't need to make any big decisions urgently. I suggested an obstetric referral and she said she'd only do that if it was you she could talk to.' Grace's smile felt almost shy. 'She's terrified of obstetricians but you certainly won her over.'

Jock's shrug was modest. 'Sometimes it pays to look like an overgrown, scruffy teenager instead of a consultant surgeon, I guess. Did you talk about an elective Caesarean to avoid any re-peat trauma like the first time?'

'I did. She'd done some research herself and found some online chat that said it was really hard to find an obstetrician that would agree to it. That you either had to be diagnosed with men-tal illness to qualify or you'd be branded as "too posh to push".'

'Not true,' Jock said. 'I'll be happy to see her. Mark it as needing an urgent consult and they'll squeeze her into my next outpatient clinic. I'd be happy to do the C-section myself if that's the best choice for her and I'd do my absolute best to make sure she gets a birth experience that won't end up giving her nightmares.'

'Like Melissa did this morning,' Grace said. 'I popped in to see her before I came home and she's so happy. Over-the-moon happy. It was a joy to be there.'

Grace was smiling properly this time. It hadn't been only the patients that Jock had impressed today. Not that she was about to tell him how much she'd been won over by the heart-melting moment when this obstetrician had welcomed the arrival of Melissa's baby. And—even more—by the way he hadn't hesitated to stop and help some-one in distress, as he had with Stella. He wasn't simply an excellent surgeon, was he? He was a really, really nice guy.

Quite possibly the nicest guy she'd ever met.

And that made sense, seeing as his twin sister was the best friend she'd ever made.

Jock didn't see her smile because he hadn't turned around from tending to the sausages.

He shrugged off the compliment too. 'Good to hear. I hope we get to share many more success stories like that. Now…are you ready to eat?'

'I'm starving.'

'Excellent. Come with me.'

Grace chose Dijon mustard as a condiment to go with her sausages rather than the tomato sauce Jock preferred.

Classy…

'I think you cook sausages even better than fish,' Grace said.

'I'll put that on my CV.' Jock grinned. 'It might be useful one day.'

'What for?'

'Oh, I dunno. A dating site profile?'

Grace simply shook her head as she took another bite of her dinner.

'That reminds me,' he said. 'I got a text to say that there's a few people from work going to the pub later tonight. I thought I might go along. Why don't you come too? It'd be a good chance to meet some more people.'

'Is it a work thing?'

'No. Just social. You'll know a few of them by now, like Mandy—she probably did Stella's ultrasound today.'

'Yes, she did.'

'And Dan might come.' Jock kept his tone casual. 'You met him this morning when he did Melissa's epidural.'

'Mmm.' The sound was noncommittal.

'He's single,' Jock added.

His observation was met with a raised eyebrow. 'And...?'

He held up his hands, excusing himself. 'Hey... I was the teenager with ginger hair and freckles. I thought all women were automatically attracted to the tall, dark and brooding type of guy.'

'Been there, done that.' Grace's tone was light but dismissive. 'Have no intention of ever doing it again.' She got up to take her plate to the kitchen sink. 'Thank you for that. It was delicious.'

Well...that squashed any thought that there might have been a spark between his new flatmate and his fishing buddy. It also reminded Jock that Jenni had told him Grace hadn't dated anyone since she'd escaped a bad marriage some years ago. Thinking of his sister also reminded him of her decree not to even think about hitting on Grace.

As if he would...

Having her here was almost like having Jenni

here. Another sister. He should be making sure she *didn't* hook up with anyone in a hurry instead of pushing her towards his single friends. Especially if she was still vulnerable in the wake of a failed relationship. But that had been years ago, hadn't it? Wouldn't it be a lot healthier for her if she moved on?

Jock scraped his plate clean and got up to take it to the bench, where Jenni was now washing up.

'Here you go.' He put the plate down on the side of the bench with the other dirty dishes. Without thinking, he touched Grace's shoulder with his other hand in something between a gentle squeeze and an appreciative pat. 'Thanks...'

He felt the jerk beneath his hand but what was more shocking was that the clean plate Grace was lifting from the hot, soapy water got dropped— almost thrown—to the floor, where it shattered into sharp fragments.

'Oh, *no*...' Grace put her hand to her mouth. 'I'm so sorry...'

She barely glanced up at Jock but that split second of time was still long enough to make Jock freeze. Because he could see the same kind of flash that he'd seen earlier today—in Stella's eyes.

Fear...

'Hey... It's okay.' Jock wanted to offer Grace a hug, but that would obviously be completely the wrong thing to do when it had been touching her in the first place that had caused this. 'It's me that should apologise. I gave you a fright.'

Grace peeled off some paper towels from the roll and crouched to start picking up pieces of broken crockery.

'It's not your fault. It's…'

Oh, God… Was that a tear he could see rolling down Grace's cheek?

Jock crouched beside her. 'It's okay, Grace,' he said softly. 'You're perfectly safe…'

She stopped picking up the shards. She stopped moving at all.

'You know, don't you?' she whispered. 'Did Jenni tell you?'

'Jenni didn't tell me anything,' Jock said. 'Only that you got out of what she said was an awful marriage a long time ago.'

Grace didn't say anything.

'Did he hit you, Grace?' Jock asked very quietly. 'That bastard that you were married to?

Very slowly, Grace lifted her chin, just enough to be able to raise her gaze to meet his. She didn't have to say anything at all because he could see the answer to his question in her eyes.

And something cracked in his chest. He hadn't felt this angry on someone else's behalf—or so determined to protect them—since…since some bullies had had a go at Jenni on their very first day at primary school. He'd only been five years old but he'd been fast and fierce enough to fight for his sister.

'You're safe,' he told Grace again. 'You'll always be safe with me.'

And this time it was a promise.

CHAPTER FOUR

JOCK DIDN'T REPEAT the suggestion that Grace went to the pub with him.

He didn't even go himself. Instead, he unearthed a bottle of wine from a kitchen cupboard, as Grace finished clearing up in the slightly awkward aftermath of her hurling that plate onto the floor.

'You're not on call tonight, are you?'

'No.' Grace picked up the cutlery to dry.

'Neither am I.' Jock held up the bottle. 'Do you like red wine?'

'Sometimes.'

'Would now be one of those times, do you think?'

Grace could feel her lips curving into a smile, which was really surprising given how discombobulated she was feeling right now. How mortifying was it that she'd overreacted to that casual male touch like that? How vulnerable had it made her feel that Jock had guessed one of her darker secrets?

But how much more vulnerable was she feeling in the wake of him telling her that she was safe?

Because she really, really wanted to believe him.

She *did* believe him—as far as being in his company was concerned, anyway.

Grace caught her lip between her teeth, catching the smile that was trying to wobble free as she dried her hands on the tea towel and turned towards Jock.

'Now would definitely be one of those times,' she said.

They went outside to sit on the wicker chairs and watch the sky take on enough of a pretty pink tinge for it to reflect on the sea. The day seemed to be taking a breath and releasing it in a sigh of relief that Grace could feel right down to her bones. She let out her own soft sigh as she sank into the cocoon of old cushions and for a quiet minute or two they simply sat there watching the colours deepen before they began to fade. It was Grace who finally broke the silence.

'Can you tell which boat is *Lassie* from this distance?'

'I can. There aren't that many clinker-built boats in the marina. Most people prefer flashy fibreglass hulls because they're much easier to maintain.'

'Does clinker mean it's made out of wood?'

'It's a type of building with wood. The planks in the hull overlap each other. It's probably the oldest and best-known technique of boat building.' Jock made an appreciative sound. 'I fell in love with it when I was a kid. When I got to play on a pond in this ancient dinghy with peeling paint and a seat that gave you splinters. I learned to row in that boat, which was quite an achievement given that the water was only about knee-deep.'

'Was that the boat you pushed Jenni out of?'

Jock paused as he was reaching for the wine bottle to top up their glasses. 'She told you about that?'

Grace nodded.

'It's not true,' Jock growled. 'She was leaning over the side of the boat because she thought she could see a fish. I was actually trying to catch hold of her before she fell in.'

That seemed perfectly believable, coming from a man who could look at you as if he was prepared to fight dragons to protect you.

A man who could tell you that you would always be safe as long as you were with him.

A man whose smile—like the one Grace was getting now—seemed to make everything a bit brighter. Shiny, even...

The tendril of sensation flickering through her body could have been misinterpreted as attraction but it was easy to reassure herself that it was nothing more than the warmth of a developing friendship.

If it was anything else she wouldn't feel this safe, would she?

'But then she stood up and I knew she was okay,' Jock said, 'but she looked like a drowned rat and she was so cross that it was funny. I think she decided I'd pushed her because that was less embarrassing than her just falling out. She's never forgiven me for laughing at her so much.'

'Oh, I think she has. She adores you.' Grace took a slow sip of her wine. Of course she did. Who wouldn't?

'I was an only child,' she confessed. 'I would have given anything to have had a brother—even if they did push me out of a boat.'

Jock laughed. 'Be careful what you wish for,' he said. 'I could arrange for that to happen, you know.'

This silence that fell as dusk deepened around them felt even more companionable. Grace could even forget the embarrassment of someone knowing that she'd been in an abusive relationship. At least he didn't know that she'd been weak enough to stay in it for far too long. Or why...

'Did Jenni tell you that the boat incident happened when we were in a foster home? Just for the long school break in summer. Our mother couldn't cope with school holidays when she had to work and social services didn't seem to like a pair of twins being left to fend for themselves for weeks on end.'

Had Jock sensed the direction her thoughts were straying? Or did he want to make her feel less exposed by sharing something of his own that was personal?

Grace's nod was hesitant. She would never have pushed him into talking about a childhood she knew had been a lot less than ideal, but perhaps this was a chance to let him know that the safety he'd offered her went both ways. And that it was something that felt very unexpected. And very special.

'We only spoke about it once. I'm pretty sure there might have been some wine involved on that occasion as well. Jen said it was one of the better foster homes you had to spend time in. Because you got to be there together...' Grace needed to wash away the lump in her throat with another mouthful of wine. 'I'm so sorry you guys had things to deal with that no kids should have to, but you must be so proud of each other and how far you've come since then.'

Jock's gaze was steady. 'It leaves scars,' he said quietly.

'Of course it does.' Grace offered Jock a smile. 'And it's so much worse when you get those scars when you're too young. Most of us collect a few scars along the way later in life, but when you're a kid you should be protected. Wrapped in the kind of love that can kiss so many things better.'

Jock's breath came out in a huff that told her he'd never been wrapped in that kind of love.

'I learned two things,' he said. 'That broken promises can feel like the end of the world. Like the promises our mother would make that we kept believing, even when we knew we shouldn't. Like the one about never having to go somewhere else in the holidays. Or that her new relationship would make us a real family because she was *in love* and he loved her back and that everything was going to be perfect from now on...' Jock cleared his throat. 'I decided when I was about ten years old that I would never, ever make a promise I couldn't keep. And I never will.'

'I knew you could be trusted before I even met you,' Grace said. 'Jenni said you're the only person on earth that she would trust with her life.'

Jock smiled. 'Siblings and friends.' He nodded. 'The only kind of love that can be trusted. That was the other thing I decided. Jenni and I saw our mother lurching from one disaster to another and we gave up hoping that everything would ever be perfect. When we were about thirteen we both made a solemn vow that we would never get married. I don't know about Jenni, but I also decided that I was never going to fall in love because that was how the worst disasters always started.'

'That explains a lot,' Grace said. 'I thought Jenni was just super fussy when it came to boy-friends. That she'd find "the one" if she kissed enough frogs. But I wasn't really joking this morning when I said that the current model might be getting near his expiry date, so she shouldn't waste her money on a weekend with him in Portugal.'

'And she accuses me of breaking hearts?' Jock let his breath out in a huff. 'I'm very careful that I don't do that. I make it absolutely clear right from the start that it's never going to be anything serious. To be honest, I don't think I'm capable of falling in love.'

'Really?'

'The risk is way too big.' Jock shrugged. 'If you build your whole world around trusting that someone else feels the same way you do, you give them the power to destroy everything.'

'That is true,' Grace said softly. She knew that, so how could she disagree?

'At least it's safe enough to love your friends and siblings. Much harder to break those bonds—even if you live on opposite sides of the world.'

'I don't think Jenni really believes that you go around breaking hearts. She did, however, suggest

ALISON ROBERTS

that the only long-term commitment you were likely to make was to your boat.'

The sound from Jock was one of amusement now. 'And she told me that you were so out of bounds she'd never speak to me again if I even thought about breaking the rules.'

Grace didn't have to confess that Jenni knew she couldn't handle being touched by men since she'd escaped her marriage. Jock had already found that out the hard way, hadn't he?

'There was another part of that vow we made to never get married,' Jock added. 'We both said we never wanted to have kids. In case they ended up like us. Living with those broken promises and catching the fallout of the disastrous new relationships.' He held Grace's gaze. 'We were hiding out down by the canal at the time. Keeping out of the way of a stepfather who liked to hit us.'

The look Grace was receiving from Jock was telling her that he got it. That he knew what it was like to have someone that hurt you physically, but she could sense the undercurrent of empathy that went deeper. That advertised an understanding of how deep the emotional scars that got left behind could be.

And then his face lightened and that cheeky grin emerged again. Clearly, it was time to step out of the shadows that dark memories caused.

Grace suspected this was a defence mechanism that Jock had learned to apply at a very early age.

'So…when are you going to come out fishing with me? We can talk about how we're going to lure Jenni out here. If she just came for a visit, I'm sure we could persuade her to emigrate. Let's make it the next day off we have that coincides.' His grin widened. 'That should give me enough time to plan my strategy for pushing you overboard when you least expect it…'

If Grace was bothered by the prospect of being pushed off his boat, she certainly wasn't showing it. She was looking a lot more relaxed about life in general, in fact, as the days following his teasing threat ticked past. Even better, she hadn't tried to revisit any part of what they'd discussed that evening.

Jock had been a bit shocked at himself, to be honest, for having discussed his childhood at all. There was only one other person on the planet that he'd ever talked to about it and it had to be a good ten years or more since it had come up in any conversation with Jenni. By tacit agreement, they were moving forward with their lives and neither of them wanted to revisit a past they'd worked so hard to deal with and leave behind.

And he hadn't told Grace everything. He'd let her assume that he and Jenni had vowed not to have children because of physical abuse they'd had to face, but that hadn't been the worst of it. The deepest wounds hadn't been inflicted by a stepfather or any 'uncles' that joined their family for any length of time. No…those scars had been left by the twins' mother.

Being told so often that their arrival in the world—and their continued existence—had ruined her life.

The shame of feeling unwanted had seeped into every cell before they'd been old enough to know that it wasn't their fault. On some level they believed they weren't good enough to be loved by anyone other than each other, but that had been enough to survive and nobody else ever had to know. It was just another part of the past that was never talked about and never would be.

Jock was happy enough with his life now that he wouldn't want to change anything. So happy, he had moments when the past might have never even existed, but he didn't regret what he *had* said to Grace.

Especially that she was safe.

It felt like he was protecting Jenni all over again, but with the wisdom and strength that all his life experiences had given him it was not only easy—automatic, almost—it was a genuine pleasure.

And somehow, what had happened that evening had created a connection with Grace that Jock had never had with anyone other than his sister and that was…

It was nice, that's what it was.

He had promised that Grace was safe with him, but he hadn't expected to start feeling that *he* was safe with *her*.

And why wouldn't he?

The person *he* trusted the most in the world trusted Grace and Jenni's instincts about people had always been spot on.

But it was also partly due to her not raising the subject of their conversation again—respecting his privacy in the same way he was guarding hers. No one should ever intrude on a space like that without an invitation.

Maybe she'd forgotten all about the threat of being pushed overboard from *Lassie*'s deck—or even the promised fishing trip, given that it was proving difficult to find a day they were both off work and not on call.

But that was okay.

He had a fishing trip lined up with Dan for his next day off, a job he loved every minute of and a flatmate who was as easy to be around as his own sister and had the promise of becoming one of those friendships that could last a lifetime.

And life didn't really get much better than this, did it?

CHAPTER FIVE

ONE BUSY DAY led into another and Grace didn't mind juggling her rosters and postponing her scheduled days off to fill gaps left by the ongoing staff shortages in the maternity department of Picton Hospital, even if it meant she still hadn't been out on Jock's boat.

The jigsaw puzzle pieces of her new life were coming together to form a picture that was reminiscent of the dreams that had been sparked by Jenni's suggestion that Grace came to work in a small country at the very bottom of the world.

She wasn't a stranger here any longer. She was making new friends at work and the kind of connections that were created by cases that were shared. Grace worked with other midwives, obstetricians, anaesthetists and technicians during births and liaised with GPs, practice nurses and others in her antenatal and postnatal care of mothers.

Some of those connections were going to become stronger as time went on. Like the one she had with Jock that Stella Watson had created. Grace was delighted to hear that she'd been added to an outpatient clinic within days of her running away from her first midwife appointment.

'I told her that a planned C-section was not only possible but, in her case, advisable,' Jock reported. 'Her physical and mental health—maybe even her marriage—could be at risk if she felt unable to continue with the pregnancy, when she *and* her husband really want another child. But they could be at greater risk if she goes through a pregnancy with the level of anxiety she has about giving birth again and that, in my opinion, outweighed any increased risk of having surgery.'

'What did she say?'

'She was so relieved it took about half a box of tissues before we could plan the next steps, and we didn't get very far because all she wanted to do was go and find her husband and tell him everything.'

Grace hadn't realised how worried she'd been about Stella until she felt a wash of relief that morphed into happiness. She wrapped her arms around herself as if she needed to hug someone. 'You're a bit of a star, Jock, you know that, don't you?'

Jock shrugged in what was becoming a familiar gesture to dismiss a compliment. 'I've made an appointment for them both to come in next week and we'll discuss everything.'

'Brilliant. I'll get in touch with Stella and see if I can catch her at the same time to arrange our first proper antenatal visit.'

It had been her turn to add a new strand to another connection between them a day or two after that.

'I did a postnatal home visit to see Melissa today,' she told him. 'I took her stitches out.'

'How's the wound looking?'

'Really clean. Her temperature, blood pressure and heart rate were all normal too, and she's feeling well so there's no sign of any infection.'

'How's her PV bleeding? She still had a bit of ongoing loss when I saw her just prior to discharging her.'

'It's slowed down a lot. She's keeping mobile to lower any risk of thrombosis. As much as she's allowed to, anyway. Jason's taken a few weeks' paternity leave and he's not letting her do any housework. He was hanging out the washing when I arrived.'

'And the baby?'

'Oh, she's gorgeous. They've named her Charlotte but are calling her Charlie. She's doing really well—just a touch of nappy rash. I'll visit again when Jason's gone back to work and make sure she's managing by herself. She might feel a bit isolated then. They live down a windy shingle road at the bottom of a huge hill. The house is hidden by trees and they have a tiny private beach that's even got a jetty for their boat.'

'Nice… Just the kind of property I'd love to have one day.'

Grace could imagine him there, happily pottering around with his boat or fishing off the jetty. With a couple of cute kids playing on the beach who had curly red hair and were shrieking with laughter.

Oh, no…wait… There wouldn't be any children. There wouldn't be a wife either. Because he—and Jenni—had convinced each other that was the best idea.

She could understand why they'd made that vow. Of course she could. Their mother had given them appalling evidence of how bad things could be when they went wrong. But surely they'd seen evidence of how amazing it could be when it *didn't* go wrong? Were Jock and Jenni really so sure they wanted to keep such a solid barrier in place they weren't even going to try?

If she told either of them what she thought, they would just say it was a case of the pot calling the kettle black, wouldn't they? At least she'd dreamt of a family of her own, though. And she'd done her best to make it happen. Maybe she hadn't quite given up hope that it *could* happen for herself one day. Maybe that was partly why she'd found the courage to start a completely new life.

Whatever. What was in her own past wasn't something Grace wanted to think about, much less start talking about again. So she found a smile as she raised her eyebrows.

'This is so you and *Lassie* can live happily ever after together?'

'Exactly.'

The laughter was shared but Grace felt a squeeze on her heart that was poignant enough to be almost painful.

No matter how beautiful the setting, living alone without even another house in sight would have to be heartbreakingly lonely at times. And Jock McKay was someone who really, really didn't deserve to end up being that lonely.

But he was smiling and shaking his head now, as if he'd read her thoughts and wanted to reassure her.

'Never going to happen,' he said. 'I'd never stay in one place long enough to own my own jetty.' His smile widened. 'It's much more likely that *Lassie* and I will just sail off into the sunset together.'

It had been a throwaway comment.

A joke.

Judging by the expression on her face, the prospect of sailing off into the sunset with his beloved boat was clearly not something that Grace had deemed a future worth dreaming about. She almost looked as though it might be something to feel sad about.

Jock, however, heard the echo of her words in his head again a few days later when he took Dan out for an afternoon's fishing and the contented purr of the engine as they headed out into the Sounds to see if the snapper were biting made him think that *Lassie* was quite content with his newly forming plans for their shared future. And Grace was working today so she wasn't here to give him that look again.

'How long have you been living here now, Dan?' Jock handed his friend a cold bottle of lager from the tiny fridge in *Lassie*'s galley when they dropped the anchor in one of their favourite spots.

'Longer than you, mate. Why?'

'What made you choose Picton?'

'Job came up. I needed a change.'

Dan was a man of few words, which was a desirable attribute in a fishing companion but he was quite happy to talk if someone made the effort to engage him. He was also a friend whose opinion Jock respected.

'Do you still like it here?'

Dan took a long swallow from his beer, letting his gaze rest on the idyllic scenery around them.

'Are you kidding? What's not to like? I've got no plans to leave any time soon. That's why I've bought a house here.'

Jock nodded, his smile one of complete agreement. 'We've got the best work-life balance, that's for sure. A place that's got this to offer as a playground but the town's big enough to keep work interesting. And small enough to keep us on our toes on a good day.'

In a larger city, a specialist in maternal-foetal medicine would be consulted for the management of any pregnancies with a higher-than-normal risk of complications, but here Jock had the responsibility of monitoring cases in an area of obstetric medicine that provided the kind of challenges he loved the most. A low-lying placenta, perhaps, or a history of previous miscarriages or—his favourite—a multiple pregnancy.

It was comforting to have the backup of New Zealand's capital city's medical resources being only a short flight away across the short distance between the South and North islands, and that meant that more complex cases could also be managed, with Jock as part of a team of local specialists for pregnant women with existing medical conditions like congenital heart disease, high blood pressure, diabetes or a previous organ transplant.

Jock might grumble about the workload occasionally, like when he'd been trying to persuade Jenni to apply for one of the vacant midwife positions, but he got enough downtime to know exactly how lucky he was to be living here. It was paradise for anyone who loved the sea and this part of the South Island was also a mecca for people who loved good food and wine, picturesque towns, dramatic scenery and interesting company. People who loved life and wanted to make the most of it, in fact. Like Jock did.

Was that why Dan sounded so content to stay here? Was Grace right to think that never staying long enough in one place was the wrong approach to finding lasting happiness?

What real reason did Jock have not to try putting down roots and building a life that he'd never want to leave?

Jock took a swallow of his own beer. 'Maybe I should start looking for a house to buy too,' he said cautiously, testing his thought aloud. 'Might even see if I can get one with its own jetty.'

'Sounds like a plan.' Dan's nod was approving. 'So you're not tempted to go back to Scotland?'

Jock grinned. 'And leave this behind? Are *you* kidding?'

'Don't you have a sister still there?'

'I'm working on a cunning plan to persuade her to move here. Grace is helping.'

'Grace?'

'My new flatmate. The midwife who was at that last emergency C-section we did together.'

'Ah, yes... I remember her. Blonde. Cute. Seems quite shy.'

'Cute' wasn't quite the word Jock would have chosen to describe a woman who was not only gorgeous but intelligent and clever and...caring. 'Shy' wasn't exactly appropriate either. Grace was wary. And she had reason to be.

'Blonde and cute is way more your type than mine,' Dan said dryly. 'And, come to think of it, I did notice the way she was smiling at you when you were holding that baby. And you're living with her?' He gave Jock an incredulous glance. 'So how's *that* working out so far...?'

Oh, good grief...did Dan think he was incapable of keeping his hands off a gorgeous woman?

'She's my sister's best friend,' he said firmly. 'Which puts her completely off-limits as far as I'm concerned.'

'Why?'

'It just does. It could end up messing with their friendship and my sister might never speak to me again. It was Jenni who told her about the job going here, and she made it clear that nothing was allowed to happen between us. So that's that.'

Dan's grunt sounded almost impressed. 'Good for you.'

'Anyway, Grace is talking Jenni into a trip to

come and visit. We're going to try and make sure she has such a good time she'll want to come back permanently.'

Dan smiled. 'That would definitely make life interesting. Does she like boats?'

'No. She hates them. But that's her only real flaw. She makes up for it in many other ways.'

'I'll look forward to meeting her,' Dan said. 'But I'm wondering how Picton would cope with having both the McKay twins in residence.'

'Double trouble.' Jock nodded. 'Oh—' he put his beer down hurriedly '—I've got a nibble...'

The conversation was forgotten as he began the tussle to land what felt like a big fish. A flash of colour as it came closer to the surface confirmed that it was a snapper, which was his favourite fish to eat. Fresh from the sea and cooked to perfection on the barbecue, Grace would be more than impressed with how delicious her dinner was going to be.

Maybe he'd flick Greta a text and see if she wanted to come and join them. She might have moved on because she was looking for more than he could offer but, as far as Jock knew, she hadn't found a new relationship yet. Maybe she'd like to keep their friendship going in the meantime? With those benefits they'd both enjoyed in the last couple of months?

That way, Jock would be able to end a perfect day with the perfect meal, in the company of good friends. Maybe even the bonus of overnight company?

No…

The idea was remarkably unappealing.

He didn't want Greta's company tonight, did he?

He wanted Grace's.

Not for sex, of course. But for everything else—like the companionship and conversation and…and that feeling of connection. With a frisson of foreboding, Jock realised that maybe Dan hadn't been so far off the mark when he'd given him the look that suggested he was very likely to fancy Grace.

No… He wasn't even going to think about that. That sense of connection was there because of the bond they both had with Jenni, that was all. She was another sister for Jock.

And he didn't have to think about it any longer. A distraction came in the form of a huge snapper that he managed to flip onto the deck.

'*Yes*…' Jock's shout was triumphant.

Life didn't get any better than this, did it? It wasn't perfect, but it was such a waste not to make the most of the best it had to offer when everyone knew how short life was. Moments like this. With good friends and good times. And, aye… sex *was* a part of some of the best moments Jock had ever found in life, but he wasn't going there with Grace.

He was perfectly capable of following rules when they made sense.

He did, however, feel sorry that Grace was missing what was an important part of life. As a brother, or even just as a friend, would it be possible to encourage her to be brave enough to try again?

Not with him, of course, but perhaps he could facilitate a friendship that she could trust enough to let it grow if they happened to find they liked each other? With someone who was thoughtful and patient and quite happily single, so there would be no reason to apply any pressure whatsoever for it to be more than a friendship.

Maybe that idea of setting her up with Dan shouldn't have been discarded so soon?

His mate was happily single. Jock knew he'd been married once but they'd never talked about past relationships. Or even present ones. They'd double-dated once or twice, and maybe part of their connection was due to respecting the privacy of each other's love lives. Jock certainly wasn't going to judge Dan on something as trivial as enjoying an occasional one-night stand.

But it was, in fact, possible that Dan was on the lookout for someone special to share the rest of his life with and he just hadn't met the right person yet.

And Grace Collins was certainly special…

Jock's gaze slid sideways. How easy would it be to suggest that Dan came for dinner tonight to share a meal of the fish they were catching? That way, they could meet each other properly.

No…

He didn't want to set Grace up with Dan.

He didn't want to set her up with anyone, in fact. Why would he risk putting her into a situation where she might feel uncomfortable—or worse, where she might end up getting hurt?

He'd promised she would always be safe if he was around.

And Jock never made a promise he couldn't keep.

CHAPTER SIX

ANTENATAL CLINICS WERE a favourite part of Grace's duties as a midwife. This was where she got to know the women under her care and built the relationship that was so important when it came time to play her part in the major life event that having a baby represented.

If a midwife did her job well, a mother would remember her for ever.

As a midwife, Grace could often recognise women she knew she was going to remember well before they gave birth.

Like Maureen Petersen, who hadn't given up on her dream to be a mother and had decided to do something about it on her own when she turned forty.

And Stella Watson—the first woman who had ever run away from Grace.

Stella had now entered her second trimester and, thanks to the reassurance that she would not have to go through another traumatic birth experience, was beginning to relax enough to start enjoying her pregnancy.

'I wish I'd spoken to someone a long time ago,' she confided as Grace wrapped the blood pressure cuff around her upper arm. 'Do you think six years is too big a gap between siblings?'

'I think Scott's going to be the best big brother.' Grace fitted the stethoscope to her ears and smiled at the small boy who was going through the toy box in the corner of the consulting room. 'Is it school holidays at the moment?'

Stella nodded. 'And he came to the last appointment we had with Dr McKay so he wanted to come back again. Dr Jock, he calls him.' Stella was smiling. 'To be honest, I'm not sure that talking to anyone else *would* have helped this much. There's something about Dr McKay, isn't there?'

Grace let the rest of the air out of the cuff and pulled her pen from her pocket to record the blood pressure measurement.

'There certainly is,' she agreed. 'And luckily, he's not just a nice man—he's an excellent surgeon.'

It was no surprise that Stella was now feeling safe enough to be able to cope with this pregnancy. Being anywhere near Jock was enough to make Grace feel safer than she had in longer than she could remember.

More than that, even. Thanks to the boundaries that had been put in place so firmly by Jenni, there was no threat of anything getting out of control or for either of them to think of their relationship as anything more than friends or honorary siblings. Grace had something in her life now that she hadn't realised how much she was missing.

Male companionship.

And…okay…maybe there was an element of admiration there. On both sides. But it didn't have any sexual significance. Instead, it could be enjoyed. Grace could allow herself to feel more… feminine? Feeling desirable was a step too far, but she was definitely feeling better about herself.

And she had Jock McKay to thank for that. The brother of her bestie was becoming not only an equally good friend but someone she could be proud of knowing—as much for his compassion for others as any practical skills he had as a surgeon.

Did Jock realise what a gift it was to make a pregnant woman feel safe? Not just for Stella, but for her husband and her son and the baby whose birth she might be able to look forward to instead of being terrified about.

'Everything's looking great,' Grace told Stella. 'Now…it's a bit early, so it might not work, but would you like me to see if we can hear baby's heartbeat with the Doppler?'

'Ooh…yes, please.' Stella lay back on the bed and pulled up her top to expose her belly again.

'Just don't get worried if I can't find it, okay? It doesn't mean there's anything wrong, just that it's too early.'

'I won't,' Stella promised.

Scott had abandoned the toys. 'What's a Dop-er-la?'

'It's this little device.' Grace showed him the handset and attached transducer. 'It can send out high-frequency ultrasound waves that can go through the skin and then bounce back to tell us what they've found.'

'Like dolphins?' Scott's eyes widened. 'We learned about that at school. That's how they find their food.'

'Exactly like dolphins.' Grace nodded. She held the flat head of the small transducer against Stella's abdomen. 'And do you want to know something I learned about at midwife school?'

'You went to *school*?'

'I did.' Grace moved the transducer to another spot and pressed a little more firmly. 'And when we were learning to use Dopplers, the teacher told me that dolphins really love to be around pregnant women because they can hear the heartbeat of both the mother and the baby. They might even be able to *see* the baby.'

'Is that really true?' Stella asked.

'Apparently,' Grace said. She smiled. 'But even if it's exaggerated it's still another good reason to love dolphins, as far as I'm concerned.' Her smile widened at what she could hear from the speaker built into the handset of her device—the rapid beats that sounded like muffled horses galloping past. 'Can you hear that, Scott? That's your little brother or sister's heart that's making that sound.'

Stella had her fingers pressed to her mouth and tears in her eyes as she looked up at Grace. Things had just become even more real. But joy was winning over trepidation.

Jock would be just as delighted as she was at this development in a case that could have gone in a very different direction.

'Where's your phone?' she asked Stella. 'Shall we record this so you can take it home for Dad to listen to later?'

It was Scott who proudly took charge of the phone with its new audio clip as they left a short time later and Grace welcomed her last appointment for this clinic.

This was the second time Grace was seeing Tessa, who was nearly thirty weeks pregnant with twins. As it was a multiple birth, Tessa was already under the care of the obstetric department as a higher-risk pregnancy, but she had chosen to work with a midwife as well for antenatal visits that were more frequent than the normal routine but, because the twins were currently both in a breech position, Tessa was scheduled for an elective Caesarean at around thirty-seven weeks gestation as the safest option for delivery of her babies.

'Did you manage a urine sample?'

Tessa rolled her eyes. 'I need to pee constantly. Catching a bit of it is the least of my problems.'

She handed over the specimen jar and Grace unscrewed the bright yellow lid to put the dipstick into the liquid.

'Jump on the scales for me, Tessa, and then hop up on the bed and we'll do all our usual checks.'

'Jump?' Tessa laughed. 'And *hop*? Being able to do either of those things is becoming a distant memory.'

Grace smiled. Tessa's belly was certainly an impressive size. 'I'm not surprised you're feeling the need to pee frequently,' she said. 'Your uterus is the size of a full-term singleton pregnancy already and it will be putting a fair bit of pressure on your bladder.'

Grace noted a small increase in the level of protein in the urine sample but it wasn't enough to be a concern.

'Oh, my God…' Tessa was staring down at the numbers on the screen of the digital scales. 'I'm the size of a whale.' Tessa was pulling off her shoes. 'Look at that—I don't have ankles any longer. They've turned into *cankles*.'

'You have got a bit of swelling,' Grace agreed. 'But walking will help with that. Getting your feet up above the level of your heart for a decent stretch of time is good, and try and sleep on your left side at night.'

'What does that do?'

'It improves blood flow, which can reduce the swelling in the ankles and legs. You've got quite a lot more blood circulating in pregnancy and the pressure of the uterus doesn't just make the bladder overreactive, it can interfere with blood trying to get back from the legs to the heart and lungs.'

'Is it dangerous?'

'If it gets any worse, or you have symptoms like headaches or blurry vision, then you need to get checked as soon as possible because it can be a sign of pre-eclampsia. Have you had anything like that?'

'No. I just feel tired all the time. And a bit short of breath.' Tessa had managed to climb onto the bed without difficulty. She pulled the stretchy fabric of her maternity jeans down and then rubbed the enormous, pale mound with its dramatic, dark central line and the more randomly scattered red stretch marks. 'At least they've settled down today. They kept me awake half the night with what felt like a game of rugby going on.'

'Oh?' Grace placed the edge of one hand on the top of Tessa's belly to find the top of the uterus. 'Have the movements been what you're used to since then?'

'There still seems to be a lot of kicking.'

Grace used both hands on either side of the belly as she began to apply gentle pressure. She could feel the kick of a baby's foot against her hand almost instantly. 'What are you two up to in there, huh? Having a bit of a party?'

She moved her hands down slowly and systematically towards the lower uterus.

'Hmm…'

'What is it?' Tessa sounded anxious.

'I'm just going to check that again. Sometimes it's hard to tell the difference between a bottom and a head, especially when the space is getting more cramped and the babies are active.'

Grace had felt these two babies only a couple of weeks ago when there were two round, firm shapes of their heads in the upper uterus and the softer shapes of their buttocks pointing downwards. Yes…she could only find one head near the fundus now. One shape that she could 'ballot' by pushing gently from one side to the other between her fingers. She couldn't be entirely sure what she was feeling with the other twin, however, which could indicate a transverse position where it was lying more sideways than head down.

'I think one of your babies has turned around,' she told Tessa. 'That could well have been what the gymnastics you could feel last night were all about.'

'Really? Oh…' Tessa's eyes widened. 'Does that mean I might not have to have a Caesarean?'

'I'm not saying that.' Grace shook her head. 'It would be entirely up to your obstetrician to make that kind of call. What we need to do is to find out whether I'm right first and confirm which twin it is who's moved. In fact…' She glanced at her watch. 'We might go and see if we can find an ultrasound room and a technician who's not too busy.'

The radiography department which housed X-ray, MRI and ultrasound facilities was between the outpatient department and the emergency department and could also be accessed from the main reception area in the hospital foyer.

There was a pharmacy, gift shop, florist and a café adding to the busy ambience of the hospital's entrance. As Grace walked into the area with Tessa, she saw Stella and Scott coming out of the café to head towards the main doors. Coming from the opposite direction, she saw Jock coming from the emergency department.

'Jock McKay's the obstetrician you're under, isn't he?'

Tessa nodded.

'Wait here for a tick. I'll just try and catch him and let him know what's happening today.'

Jock looked as though he was heading for the café. Grace was watching the delight on Scott's face as he noticed 'Dr Jock' approaching and stopped following his mother. To her astonishment, when Scott held his arm straight up like a 'stop' signal, Jock high-fived him and then they both made fists with their hands and bumped them together. As Grace arrived, they were doing a pretend 'explosion' where they jerked their hands back and wiggled their fingers.

Scott's grin stretched from ear to ear, ignoring Stella, who was looking embarrassed that Jock had been ambushed and signalling her son to catch up with her.

'Is that a secret handshake?' Grace's voice was a stage whisper.

Scott nodded importantly.

'Don't tell anyone,' Jock warned.

'I won't,' Grace promised. She bit back her smile but that small demonstration of how good Jock was with kids had been noted. When she had time later, she would add it to the list of reasons why he didn't deserve to be alone. Or lonely.

She might have to add a degree of perception

as well. She saw the tiny frown that told her Jock could sense that she wanted a quiet word.

'Your mum's waiting for you,' Jock told Scott. 'See you next time.' His gaze caught Grace's. 'Got time for a café coffee? Or some cake? I missed lunch…'

She shook her head. 'I'm just finishing my antenatal clinic and I'm with Tessa Brownlee. One of your high-risk mums? Breech twins and on the list for an elective Caesarean?'

Jock's nod was terse. He was fully focused as he listened to why Grace was heading to the radiography department with Tessa.

'I'm just hoping there's a technician available,' she finished. 'Otherwise, I might wait with her. If you had time to call in an urgent request, that would probably help.'

Jock knew just as well as she did what the implications of this could be.

'We just need a machine that's free.' He had already turned his back on the café with its tempting coffee and cake. 'I can do the ultrasound.'

'So Twin A, who's closer to the cervix and most likely to be born first, is still breech, but Twin B has turned around to be cephalic?'

Jenni's face filled the screen of Jock's laptop that was open on the small table between the chairs on the veranda. She'd slept late on her day off and was still in bed when she answered this video call, a mug of breakfast coffee in hand.

'Yes. It was Grace that picked it up on palpation. I confirmed it with the ultrasound.'

'Told you she was good at her job, didn't I?'

'You did indeed. And you weren't wrong.'

Grace leaned in so that Jenni could see her as well as Jock. 'She thought it meant she wouldn't need to have an elective Caesarean and could at least try for a vaginal birth.'

'I guess it could.' Jenni seemed more than happy to be talking work on her day off. 'What are the odds that Twin B will be able to turn around as well?'

'There's still time for that to happen,' Jock said. 'But we're going to keep a close eye on them with frequent scans from now on.'

'Manual cephalic version's not a good idea with twins, is it?'

'It's feasible but there's not enough evidence of its efficacy or safety yet. We'll see what happens naturally in the next few weeks.'

'I'm going to be checking frequently for any signs that she might be going into labour,' Grace added. 'She lives in a bay that's not far away from town but it can only be accessed by boat, which complicates things. She wasn't that happy when Jock told her she might need to be admitted for the last week or so, so she'd be close to definitive care.'

'Did you tell her about the risk of locked twins? Even though it's rare?'

'Jock did that so well,' Grace said. 'He managed to get the message across without terrifying the poor woman.'

Her smile told Jock she had appreciated the care he'd taken.

'It *is* terrifying.' Jenni took a sip of her coffee. 'Someone was telling me a horror story just the other day. Primigravida went into a precipitous labour, came into hospital with the body of the breech twin already delivered—legs hanging out and the classic chin lock with the second twin.'

'Worst-case scenario,' Jock muttered.

'They did an emergency C-section but it was too late.' Jenni was shaking her head sadly. 'They lost both babies...'

Jock turned his head to catch Grace's gaze. They were so close together, trying to stay visible to Jenni while they shared the chat that their heads were almost touching. Jock had never been quite this physically close to her.

He'd never noticed that the colour of her eyes changed so much in different lights. The last of the daylight was fading as they sat out here to get the best reception for the call, but it might have been anxiety that was making Grace's eyes appear such a dark shade of blue. So dark they made the gold of her hair look like a halo around her face.

If it was anxiety, he could help.

'We're not going to let that happen,' he said quietly. 'Which is why it's good that we're onto it now. We're going to be watching her like a hawk.'

'We are.' Grace was still holding his gaze. 'And she's got the best obstetrician in town, so it's all good.'

Jenni laughed. 'Look at you two, bonding over a high-risk case and telling each other how you're the best in the business.' She seemed to be leaning closer to her screen when Jock shifted his gaze. 'Is it my imagination or am I catching a vibe?'

'What sort of vibe?'

'Like there's something going on that I should know about?'

'I have no idea what you mean.' Jock's tone was deliberately puzzled but it didn't fool Jenni.

'You so do,' she told him. 'It's been obvious for weeks that you two like each other.'

'Of course we do. We're *friends*.' Grace sounded horrified. She straightened up, which increased the distance between herself and Jock. 'Flatmates. We work together—'

'As if I'd break the rules,' Jock put in before Grace could come up with any more personal reasons why the notion was so appalling. 'You know how scared I am of you, Jen.'

'Just checking.' Jenni seemed satisfied. 'It's none of my business, anyway. I'd just rather know in advance.' She made a face. 'I wouldn't want to discover I was getting in the way of the romance of the century between my brother and my bestie when I come and visit next month. That would be too weird.'

Jock ignored the teasing. 'You've booked tickets?'

'I have. Flying visit. Just for a week. I've got a friend in Australia I've promised to go and see on the way back.'

'Is Fergus coming with you?' Grace asked.

'Fergus?' Jenni laughed again. 'Who's Fergus?'

Jock shook his head. 'So that wasn't the romance of the century, then?'

'Touché,' Jenni conceded. 'Fine…let's talk travel dates instead of our love lives. You'll need to book some time off so you can come and get me from the airport. I'm flying into Christchurch. That's not too far away, is it?'

'Only a few hours' drive. Message me with all the details and I'll come down and get you if I can,' Jock promised. 'You'll love the trip back. You can do it by train or bus, but if I can get enough time off I'll drive you one way at least. Maybe we can stop in Kaikōura for a night. The mountains there drop straight down into the ocean and it's famous for whale-watching. And crayfish, which is even better than the lobster we get at home.'

'I can't wait.'

Grace tilted her head closer to Jock again. 'Neither can I,' she said. 'There's going to be so much we can do. I'll make sure I've got time off as well and we can take the ferry over to Wellington for the day and go sightseeing and shopping. It'll be a good time for vineyard tours too.'

'And fishing,' Jock suggested. 'You're going to love my new boat.'

'I'm not setting foot on your boat,' Jenni declared. 'You push people off.'

'He hasn't pushed me off yet,' Grace said. 'Oh, wait… I haven't been out on the boat. For some reason, our days off never seem to coincide.'

'I'd keep it that way if I was you. That brother of mine is not to be trusted on boats.' Jenni sighed theatrically. 'I should get up and get on with my day. And it's probably past time you two were in bed.' Her expression was pure mischief now. 'Oops. You know what I meant…'

'Bye, Jenni. Nice talking to you.' Jock slammed the laptop shut before she could say anything else. 'Sorry about that.' He made a wry face. 'She should know better than to make jokes like that. As *if*…'

Grace turned her head sharply enough to make him think he'd said too much. Was he breaking an unspoken promise that he wouldn't intrude on her privacy more than he already had?

But she was smiling at him. 'It's okay,' she said. 'Real friends never need to tread on eggshells. 'Night, Jock.'

'Night, Grace. Sleep well.'

He watched her walking towards the front door to go back inside the house. He was happy he hadn't upset her, but those two words were still hanging in the air.

As *if*…?

What had he meant by that, exactly? It wasn't as if he found Grace unattractive, was it? Far from it. She was the perfect woman.

It wasn't as if he wouldn't be delighted if she found the courage to get back into the dating game either. Grace deserved to find the very best of everything life had to offer.

It was just the idea of them being attracted to each other that had been so far out of the question he hadn't even considered it to be a possibility. If only he'd said something that had captured how he really felt instead of just dismissing it so blatantly. He could say something now but he hesitated, wondering if he might end up making things even more awkward, and the opportunity vanished.

Maybe they could just pretend it hadn't happened? Or that it was no big deal?

It didn't need to affect their friendship, did it?

Grace was about to disappear through the door but turned her head slightly at the last moment, as if she felt Jock watching her. It was no more than a fleeting glance that barely lasted longer than a heartbeat, but it left Jock with the impression that Grace knew exactly what he was thinking.

Because she was thinking about the same thing?

CHAPTER SEVEN

IT HADN'T BEEN INTENTIONAL, of course, but there was no denying that Jenni was responsible for this…

This…what was it?

Awkwardness?

Or maybe it was a different level of awareness. Of each other.

It *wasn't* attraction. Grace hadn't had even a frisson of sexual attraction to any man since her marriage had ended and if it ever happened—which was highly unlikely—her best friend's brother certainly wouldn't be a contender, no matter how highly she regarded him or how much she loved his company or even how safe she felt around him. Jenni had hit the nail on the head when she'd deemed that possibility simply 'too weird'.

But Jenni's light-hearted suggestion there might be a sexual undercurrent to their friendship had changed something. Eye contact was suddenly uncomfortable. Spending time alone together was something to be avoided. The fact that they were living together was starting to feel like it was becoming a problem.

The obvious solution was to talk about it. To share a private joke even, about how ridiculous it was. If anyone could make Grace laugh about how she'd practically thrown a plate at him when he'd barely touched her, it would be Jock McKay. But the time to have done that easily had slipped away and, as one day morphed into the next, it was proving surprisingly difficult to find the right moment to say anything at all. Was that because she didn't want to make things any worse?

The way he'd said 'As *if...*'

As if he wouldn't be remotely interested in Grace even if she was the last woman on the planet?

It seemed as if they had somehow agreed it would be better to say nothing at all and pretend it hadn't happened. But that wasn't working, was it?

Even catching sight of Jock at the other end of the ward corridor took something off the shine Grace felt, leaving a very tired but ecstatic young couple to spend some time with the beautiful baby she'd just helped deliver just as dawn was breaking.

It was a relief to turn into the sluice room to

deal with the dirty linen she'd taken out of the delivery room. She wouldn't have to avoid eye contact that was even a nanosecond too long. Or find something to talk about that was purely professional—just in case it could be interpreted as being...*too* friendly?

Despite her assurance that their friendship was real enough for them to not worry about walking on eggshells, that seemed to be exactly what they were both doing and it was bothering Grace. Squeezing sanitiser onto her hands after putting the linen into the appropriate laundry bag, she came to the conclusion that something had to be done about this.

She was going to find Jock and talk to him.

Determined to do it before she could change her mind, Grace pulled open the sluice room door and walked out—straight into the path of someone heading for the ward's reception area.

Someone she knew.

'Yvonne? Is everything all right?'

Grace had seen Yvonne at an antenatal clinic only days ago and she'd been filled with excitement because she'd felt the first movements of her baby, eighteen weeks into her pregnancy.

She wasn't looking excited right now, however. She looked pale and...frightened. The man walking beside her looked just as distressed.

'We didn't know where to go,' he said. 'Our GP's clinic doesn't open for hours and Evie's bleeding...'

'Come with me.' Grace led the young couple to a delivery suite that she knew was unoccupied. A private space.

'Tell me what's been happening,' she said.

'I woke up because of the cramps,' Yvonne said. 'And I thought I'd wet myself but...but then David turned on the light and...' She squeezed her eyes shut and stifled a sob.

David was perched on the side of the bed, his arm around his wife. 'It was blood,' he said. 'Watery blood.'

'Are you still getting the cramps?'

'No.'

'Still bleeding?'

'I don't think so.'

'We'll check. And I'll find a portable ultrasound. I think one of our obstetricians is on the ward at the moment too, so I'll have a word with him.' She took Yvonne's hand and gave it a squeeze. 'I know how scary this is but we're going to take very good care of you, okay?'

It wasn't enough but it was all Grace could promise.

She could see the fear in this first-time mother's eyes and instinct told her that it wasn't misplaced.

She recognised that fear.

Sometimes you just knew when something was terribly wrong.

He could tell something was wrong.

'What is it, Grace?'

'Are you busy?'

'I've got a theatre list starting in thirty minutes.' This felt like the first time Jock had looked at Grace properly in days and…her eyes were as dark as they'd been the other night, when he'd known she was worried for one of her mothers. He gave his head a tiny shake. 'How can I help?'

'I've just had to tell a couple that their baby's died in utero. She's eighteen weeks and it's their first pregnancy.'

'Oh, *no*…'

Late miscarriage and stillbirth were never easy cases. Jock could feel the cloak of sadness settling around his own shoulders—sadness for the baby and the family—but he had to stifle the urge to touch Grace, to put his arm around her even, and offer support for what was likely to be a very difficult day for her as well.

'I've talked about options with them. They're both distraught but they're quite certain they don't want to go home and wait for labour to start naturally. Her cervix is closed so I had to warn them it could take up to a couple of weeks. Yvonne says she couldn't even imagine doing that.'

Jock nodded. 'Let's go and see them.'

The lights in the room had been dimmed for using the portable ultrasound and clearly hadn't been turned up again. Jock found the grief-stricken mother in the arms of her husband, who was on the bed with her. Grace went to stand beside them and he saw the way Yvonne immediately reached out to hold her hand. He pulled up a chair and sat beside the bed as Grace introduced them.

'I'm so very sorry this has happened,' he said gently.

'*Why* has it happened?' Yvonne had tears streaming down her cheeks. 'What did I do wrong?'

'You haven't done anything wrong,' Jock said. 'This can happen for so many different reasons, but usually it's because of a problem with the baby's development, like a genetic abnormality or a serious problem like a heart defect. We can do tests but often a reason isn't found. I'm sorry...'

'What's going to happen now?' David's voice was raw.

'We'll give Yvonne some medication to soften the cervix and to induce labour. It might happen quite quickly or it could take a few hours. You'll stay here and you'll have someone with you at all times.'

'Me,' Grace said softly. 'I'll be here. I won't leave you.' She only came as far as the door with Jock as he went to chart and find the medications.

'Are you familiar with the local protocols and regulations?' he asked her quietly.

She nodded.

'Are you okay?'

She nodded again. 'The first postgraduate training I did was in bereavement midwifery. I know how important it is.'

'I'll come back as often as I can.'

'Thanks, Jock.' Her eyes were the darkest he'd ever seen them but there was a serenity in her body language that was reassuring. 'But don't worry. I've got this…'

From the corner of her eye, Grace saw the moment that Jock slipped quietly back into the room when he had finished in Theatre. She didn't turn around, however, because her attention was completely on Yvonne, who had given birth just a short time ago and then collapsed into her husband's arms, overwhelmed with grief.

Grace had been working quietly, taking care of what needed to be done. She had gently cleaned the baby girl and wrapped her in a soft blanket and she was standing with her back to the door, the baby in her arms, as Jock entered silently. She could actually feel the moment he sensed what was going on and went very still so that he didn't interrupt.

'Would you like to see her?'

Yvonne had her head buried against David's shoulder, her face hidden. He had his head bent over hers, his eyes closed.

Grace knew how scared they both were of this moment. 'It's okay,' she whispered. 'There's nothing to be afraid of.'

Yvonne's broken, muffled words were heartbreaking. 'But…does she look like a real baby…?'

'She looks perfect,' Grace said. She didn't have to force her smile and she knew they would be able to hear it in her tone. 'She's very tiny—just the length of my hand—but she's beautiful. She has all her fingers and toes and the sweetest little ears and nose.'

Yvonne's head was turning slowly as she listened to Grace. For a stunned moment, she stared at her daughter. And then she caught her breath in a half gasp, half sob.

'Oh…she *is* perfect…'

Grace was still smiling. 'Would you like to hold her?'

She had to blink back her own tears as she put the tiny bundle in Yvonne's arms.

'You can have as long as you want with her,' she said.

'Can we do some of the things you talked

about?' David asked as Grace turned away. 'The handprints and the photos...?' He choked up and drew Yvonne closer into his arms, his gaze fixed on his daughter.

'I'll get everything ready,' Grace promised. 'I'll leave you alone for a little while but I won't be far away. If you need me back just ring the bell.'

Jock had already opened the door, slipping out as unobtrusively as he'd entered, leaving the door open for Grace. He was waiting outside and, for the first time in days, there was nothing awkward about the eye contact they made with each other.

If anything, it felt like a statement that anything that had been interfering with the bond they had—as colleagues and friends—was irrelevant. Apart from possibly making that bond even stronger, because this situation was making it obvious how much it was valued.

There were tears in Jock's eyes and a depth of emotion that totally mirrored her own. Without even thinking about it, Grace did what she could see he needed. She gave him a hug.

Just a quick, almost fierce squeeze, which she hadn't realised she needed as much as he did until he squeezed her back after a moment's stunned immobility.

And that was that. He dropped his arms the instant he felt her loosen her hold. They both wiped their eyes and got on with what needed to be done.

'How did the birth go?'

'As well as it could have gone.'

'Pain control?'

'A bit of gas and air was all she needed.'

Placenta?'

'Delivered. Intact.'

'Do you need me for anything?' Jock asked.

'Not at the moment, but I expect they'll have more questions later. About the tests or how likely it is to happen again, maybe.'

'I'll be here. Just page me.' Jock turned to leave, but then paused. He caught Grace's gaze again. 'You're brilliant at this,' he told her quietly. 'And you're doing something that will make a real difference.'

His voice dropped to no more than a whisper. This was a personal, rather than a professional comment. 'I just wanted you to know that.'

CHAPTER EIGHT

BY THE TIME Grace got home she was done.

So drained it felt like a marathon to keep putting one foot in front of the other to get through the gate and up the path towards the house.

Jock was sitting on the top step. Waiting for her?

Watching her carefully as she came closer.

She could feel the weight of his gaze as if it was a hug. A gesture of caring.

He didn't ask how she was but the tone of his odd words made it sound as if that was his intention. 'Get changed,' he told her. 'Into your oldest, comfiest clothes. I'm taking you out.'

Grace shook her head. All she wanted to do was have a shower and go to bed. She wasn't hungry and she was beyond exhausted.

'Thanks, Jock, but I really don't want to go anywhere.'

He was getting to his feet as she walked past him. 'You want to go where I'm taking you,' he said quietly. 'Trust me. *Please...?*'

Trust…

She did trust Jock. She'd felt safe with him from almost before she'd met him, thanks to him being Jenni's brother. The weirdness of the last few days, after Jenni's left-field comment, seemed to have evaporated in the intensity of today's events and…if there was ever a time that Grace needed to trust someone to make her feel safe—and cared for—surely it was right now?

'Okay,' she sighed. 'Whatever…'

She put on her oldest pair of jeans, a tee shirt and some well-worn sneakers. She picked up a cardigan, even though the day had been a late summer scorcher because she had no idea what time she might get home and the nights could get chilly.

Jock's nod was approving when she came out of her room. He was waiting near the door with a rucksack dangling on his back and a big box in his arms.

'Can you grab the bag in the kitchen?' he asked. 'It's got the bait in it, along with some other chilled stuff.'

'Bait?'

'Aye…' Jock's nod was satisfied. 'You're finally going to go fishing. Come on…we need to get to where we're going before it starts to get dark.'

Fishing…?

It was the last thing Grace would have ever

thought she would want to do, but she was too bone-weary and drained to even summon a protest. She followed Jock down to the marina and along the pier and climbed onto his boat and just sat there as he got everything ready and then started the engine and took them out to sea.

The water was calm and the breeze a welcome relief from the heat of the day and there was nothing that Grace needed to do. She could just sit in the back of the boat on one of the wooden seats over the storage bins, her arms resting on the polished wooden side rail, watching the houses of Picton receding and the inviting inlets created by the complicated coastline around them.

If she turned her head she could see the solid shape of Jock's back as he stood nearby in the covered area of the boat with his hands on the wheel as he navigated their path, but it was more appealing to trust that he knew where he was going and simply watch the white foam of the wake the propellor was creating as it spread out in an endless V behind the boat.

Jock clearly did know where they were going because he slowed the boat and took them into a narrow channel that led to a small bay. Tall trees and the punga ferns that grew beneath them reached right down to the rocks at each end of the bay, but in the centre there was a tiny pebbled beach and when Jock had killed the engine and dropped the anchor it was so quiet Grace could hear the wash of almost non-existent waves rolling over the stones between the calls of the birds.

'Hear that?' Jock lifted one of the seats in the back of the boat to reveal fishing supplies. 'That's a bellbird.'

'It's beautiful.'

'You might even hear kiwis when it's dark.'

'Don't we need to go home before it's dark?'

Jock shook his head. 'We can go back any time you want, but we can also stay overnight and sleep on board. The best fishing is often at dusk and dawn. Fish are more active when it's dark.'

'But what about work?'

'We'll get up early enough to get some fishing in and get back in time for work. Or we can watch the sunrise on our way back.'

It sounded *so* peaceful.

'Okay…' Grace put her chin down on her arms and closed her eyes. She still wasn't excited at the thought of trying to catch a fish, but the serenity of this location was…exactly what her soul needed.

This was a gift. For her.

She opened her eyes. 'Thanks, Jock,' she said quietly. 'This is…perfect.'

He looked up from baiting a hook. 'It'll be even better when we catch a fish so we've got something to cook for dinner.'

Jock had only baited one fishing rod. Maybe the fishing part of this expedition was only a reason to be out here and that was fine. Jock sat on the seat across the back of the boat, at right angles to Grace, and flicked the hook into water that was as calm as the proverbial millpond. He didn't say anything else to break the sounds of the birds or the waves. One minute passed and then another and another and the peacefulness began seeping into Grace's bones.

She was the one who broke the silence in the end.

'They called her Luna,' she said, so quietly it was little more than a whisper.

Jock was still staring at where the fishing line disappeared into the water. 'I like that.'

'We got some lovely photos. And the little handprints and footprints. She'll never be forgotten.'

'Neither will you.' Jock put the handle of the fishing rod into an attachment on the back of the seat, putting the activity on autopilot as he turned towards her. 'What you did for Yvonne and David will make such a difference. They told me they couldn't have got through it without you. Yvonne said you just knew exactly the right things to say. And do...'

Grace could feel her eyes filling with tears as

she held Jock's gaze. 'You never forget,' she said softly. 'What it's like.'

She saw the muscles move in Jock's neck as he swallowed. Hard.

'It happened to *you*?'

Grace blinked back her tears. 'My baby died a few days before her due date due to cord compression.'

'Oh, God, Grace… I didn't know…'

'Of course you didn't. It's not something I talk about.'

'But…'

'It was a long time ago, Jock. Nearly ten years.' She smiled at him. 'Her name was Isla and she's the one who made me want to be able to help other mothers if the worst thing imaginable happened to them.'

Jock was looking stunned. 'You're…amazing. You know that, don't you?'

Grace shook her head. 'I'm really not,' she said. 'I only got to the point of being able to be there for others very recently. I thought that becoming a midwife and trying to stop it happening for other mothers was the biggest step I would ever be able to take.'

'I can't imagine what that was like for you.' Jock shook his head. 'How long after losing Isla did you deliver that first baby as a paramedic?'

'Nearly five years. And yeah…it was a shock,

but it was what I needed to shake me up enough to get my life back together. To find the courage I needed to get out of a bad…situation.'

'Five years…' Jock echoed. 'Had it been that bad for *that* long?' He sounded shocked.

Grace shook her head. 'It was great in the beginning. Barry was a police officer. I met him at an accident scene one night. Whirlwind romance—we got married three months after we met.' She shrugged. 'Stupid, I know, but all I ever wanted was to get married and have lots of kids so they'd have the siblings I never had. Barry wanted a family too. And for me to be a stay-at-home mum. The pregnancy was wonderful… Until it wasn't…' She swallowed hard. 'People process grief in different ways. Barry was angry. He wanted to try again right away but… I couldn't. We drifted apart and things gradually got…difficult.' Grace took a deep breath and let her gaze catch Jock's. 'Things can happen slowly,' she added. 'Slowly enough for it to become… I don't know…acceptable on some level…'

'Abuse is never acceptable,' Jock said quietly. 'On any level.'

'No…'

But Grace broke the eye contact with Jock abruptly. She didn't want to talk about how abusive her marriage had become. Or how she'd believed that maybe she didn't deserve to escape.

She didn't want to say anything more about losing her baby either. She wanted…

She didn't know what she wanted.

For a horrible moment, the emotions of her day and work and memories of the past threatened to destroy the peace of this place Jock had brought her to and Grace couldn't see a way out of a head space that she didn't want to fall into.

She could feel Jock watching her. It felt as though he was absorbing the struggle she suddenly found faced with.

When he spoke, his voice was serious enough to suggest he was saying something meaningful. His words were totally at the other end of the spectrum.

'Maybe this would be a good time…to push you off the boat?'

Oh, dear Lord…

What on earth had made those words come out of his mouth?

Desperation?

He'd seen how lost she was. As if she'd been hanging onto a rock to keep her from falling down an emotional cliff and she'd finally lost her grip. She was falling into some dark space he couldn't see but could imagine and…

And he had to try and catch her.

For a heartbeat he thought he'd made a terrible

mistake. He saw Grace's eyes widen and her jaw drop. Then she made a stifled sound that could have been the start of laughter. Or crying.

It was laughter. Shoulder-shaking, tear-making laughter that made Jock's tentative smile become a fully-fledged grin.

But then the laughter morphed into sobbing.

Heartbreaking, soul-scraping distress.

This was *his* fault, dammit, and Jock had no idea what to do. Until Grace held out her arms. Or maybe he was reaching towards her and she responded.

It didn't matter.

Grace wanted—*needed*—to be held and Jock was only too happy to oblige. He slid into the corner of the seat, folded Grace into his arms and held her for as long as it took for her tears to dry up. The sky took on deepening shades of pink and orange as the sun sank below the horizon and the white navigation light for an anchored vessel came on automatically. He heard the reel on the fishing rod begin to spin as a fish was hooked and then he heard it snap as the line broke and the fish fled to safety. He couldn't have cared less. *This* was why he'd thought it might be a good idea to take Grace out on the boat and he'd sit here all night holding her if that was going to make her feel even a little bit better.

But it didn't seem to take very long at all. The

sobs became hiccups and the tears became sniffing. Grace sat up and pulled up the neck of her tee shirt to mop her face.

'I'm so sorry,' she said. 'I have no idea where that came from... I haven't cried like that since...' She sniffed again. 'To be honest, I've *never* cried like that...'

'It was my fault,' Jock said apologetically. 'Offering to push you off the boat was a pretty stupid thing to say.'

But Grace shook her head. A smile began to play with the corners of her mouth. 'I've never laughed like that either,' she said. 'It feels like... I don't know...a dam burst or something.'

Jock nodded. 'It did feel like that.' He held her gaze. 'Which isn't necessarily a bad thing. How does it feel now?'

Grace's eyes might be red-rimmed and puffy but they were wide and clear and a midnight blue that was very like the darkening sea around them and Jock had never seen anything quite as lovely.

'It feels good,' Grace whispered. She looked out at the idyllic bay they were anchored in as the final tinge of colour from the sunset faded and took a deep breath. Then she smiled at Jock. 'What would you have done?' she asked. 'If I'd said yes when you offered to push me?'

'I wouldn't have pushed you,' he admitted. And then another grin finally emerged. 'Unless

I was absolutely sure it was something you really wanted me to do.'

'I think you might be the best friend I've ever had,' Grace told him. 'Only don't tell Jenni that, will you?'

'I won't,' he promised.

Grace looked back at the bay. 'It would be too cold to go swimming, wouldn't it?'

Jock shook his head. 'Only for the first sixty seconds and it would be worth it, believe me. It's almost dark, though. You'd need to stay close to the boat.'

'I can't. I don't have a swimsuit.'

'So go in your underwear. Or nothing at all. Have you ever gone skinny-dipping?

Grace looked shocked. *'No...'*

'Why not?'

'Because…it's not something I would ever do…'

'Why not?' Jock was grinning at her again. 'They say it's the things that you *don't* do that you end up regretting. What if you are sitting in a rest home when you're ninety-something and you think, *Oh... I do wish I'd gone skinny-dipping when I had the chance. Now I'll never know what it's like...'*

Grace was laughing again. 'Incorrigible,' she told him. 'That's the word for you.'

'I will if you will,' Jock said.

Grace stopped laughing. 'Can you imagine what Jenni would have to say about that?'

'I'm not going to tell her. Are you?'

Jock watched Grace biting her lip. If nothing else, at least this crazy suggestion had distracted her from any ghosts from the past. But then it was his turn to be shocked because Grace stood up. She gripped the hem of her tee shirt in both hands, ready to peel it off.

'I'm going to do it,' she said. 'Shut your eyes until I'm in the water, okay?'

Jock shut his eyes. 'Okay.'

He heard her squeak as she climbed down the ladder at the back of the boat and discovered how cold the water was when she put her foot into it. Then he heard the splash as she went in completely. Seconds later, he was also naked. He didn't bother climbing slowly down the ladder.

He just dived right in.

CHAPTER NINE

OH, MY...

The water felt like liquid crystal. Cold, clean and clear. Sharp enough to cut through anything after the initial shock of how cold it was began to wear off.

Then the feeling of the seawater touching intimate parts of her body was like nothing Grace had ever experienced in her life. She swam a little way from the boat and then stopped, treading water as she caught her breath that had been stolen by the chill. She turned to reassure herself she hadn't gone too far from the boat, just in time to see Jock poised to dive in, and her breath caught somewhere deep inside her chest all over again.

Who was this person who was swimming in the sea, completely naked—with a man? Alone with him. Nobody in the world knew where they were or what they might be doing.

Or why it was happening at all.

It felt...

It felt like exactly what Grace had wanted. She just wouldn't have been able to define it.

It felt like something brand-new. A new beginning. The real start of her new—*free*—life.

And it was amazing. Grace leaned backwards, waving her feet just enough to keep her floating. She knew her breasts were probably in full view from the glow of the white light on the back of *Lassie* but it didn't matter. Even when Jock surfaced from another dive and his head emerged right beside her.

'The stars are coming out,' she said. 'Look…'

Jock turned to float on his back as well and the silence folded itself around them for a long moment. The birdsong of dusk had ceased. Even the waves had softened enough to be inaudible as they lapped the shore.

'Did you know…' Jock said finally, his voice soft enough to not break the complete peacefulness of this moment. 'That when otters are sleeping, they hold hands so they don't float away from each other?'

'I love otters.' Grace could feel her lips curve into a smile. 'Almost as much as I love dolphins.'

'You came to live in the right place, then,' Jock said. 'You need to be near the sea. As long as you don't float away…'

Oh…

In another time and place, she could have fallen in love with someone who said something like that to her…

Grace felt his hand touching hers. A blink of time ago she would have jerked her hand away from a touch like this, as if it was hot enough to burn her skin, but…this hand belonged to a new Grace.

And the other hand belonged to Jock, who might very well be the best friend she was ever going to have.

She curled her fingers around his and for another long moment they floated together, linked like otters.

Grace couldn't think of anywhere she would rather be. Or anyone she would rather be with.

But then she suddenly shivered hard enough to make her teeth chatter.

'Time to get out,' Jock decreed. 'Or we'll get really cold.'

He twisted to get off his back, ready to swim, and the tug on her hand made Grace follow his example. They were even closer now and as she caught Jock's gaze Grace was suddenly overwhelmed with a wave of emotion.

Amazement—at where she was and how it felt as if she was finally turning a page in her life that represented a whole new beginning.

Gratitude—to Jock, for making her laugh. For making that dam burst. For…for simply being Jock.

'Thank you,' she said.

'What for?'

'This… Everything…' Words failed Grace at that point so she reached out to him instead. She was only intending to give him a quick hug, like she had in the ward earlier today when they'd left those grieving parents with their baby, but she hadn't allowed for how different it was to be in water and the way it made her whole body bump against his.

Her naked body.

Against his.

The spear of sensation that created was even more of a revelation than swimming naked had been. Maybe Jock was feeling it too, because he was looking down at Grace with an expression she couldn't read. As if words were failing him as well.

The old Grace would have turned and fled after that split second of contact.

New Grace wasn't going to make a big deal out of this.

'Thank you,' she said again. 'I'll never forget this. Being an otter…'

She let herself float just a little closer. Close enough to drop a kiss on his cheek. Or it would have been on his cheek, but Jock turned his head as she was moving and somehow her lips were brushing the corner of his mouth.

Just for a heartbeat, but that was enough.

Too much?

Grace let go, turned and swam back towards the boat.

The plan had been to catch a fish and cook fresh, beer-battered fillets for Grace. Jock had even messaged Dan to get the recipe he used for his batter and put the ingredients in the box of supplies he had carried down to the marina.

But the opportunity to catch a fish was long gone, thanks to the broken line and the time they'd spent getting thoroughly chilled by the impromptu swim. Jock had stayed in the water long enough to give Grace time to get dry and dressed in private so he was really cold by the time he clambered back on board and pulled his shorts on before he even went hunting for a towel to rub himself dry.

Grace had her cardigan on over her tee shirt but she had rolled her jeans up to her calves and her feet were still bare. She was in the galley, looking inside the box and the bag of chilled items she'd carried to the boat.

'You've got wine in here,' she said when she saw him. 'And cheese.'

'It was supposed to be an aperitif for you while

I was cooking the fish I'd caught for dinner. It might have to be baked beans on toast. Or fried eggs. You can decide while we have a glass of wine. Do you want to sit outside and see the stars for a bit longer? I can find a blanket if you get cold.'

'Definitely outside.' Grace picked up the bottle of wine. 'Can you find some glasses?'

Jock might not be providing the dinner he'd wanted to impress Grace with but she was more than happy with his choice of chilled white wine.

'This is gorgeous…like drinking velvet.'

'It's a local Pinot Gris. I'll take you to visit the vineyard one day soon. Maybe when Jenni's here.'

Grace's eyes widened.

'What's wrong? You don't like that idea?'

'We can't ever tell Jenni about tonight.' Grace took a larger gulp of her wine. 'I can't believe I even did that.'

'Don't worry. I'm not going to tell her you went skinny-dipping.' He held up his glass to touch hers. 'Cheers.'

'Cheers.'

They looked at each other over the rim of the glasses.

Jock raised an eyebrow. 'It was fun, wasn't it.'

'So much fun,' Grace agreed. 'But I still can't believe I did it. I never thought I'd ever be naked in male company again.'

Jock gave a huff of sound but couldn't find any words in response, so he refilled their glasses instead and Grace seemed just as happy to be quiet again as they sipped the wine. But, while words might have deserted him, Jock found his thoughts were as clear as the water below *Lassie*. He could remember wanting to somehow help Grace get past the barrier she had to being touched because she deserved to find the very best of what life had to offer. And he could remember saying 'As *if...*' and the look Grace had given him before she'd vanished through the door.

He was never going to get a better opportunity than this to make up for that, was he?

'Don't give up on men completely, Grace,' he said quietly. 'Don't give up on sex. Or your dream of a family. You just need to find the right person. Someone who can make you feel as special as you really are.'

Grace didn't look up immediately. She was looking down at her glass. Or maybe it was her toes? Jock looked down himself as he caught a hint of movement and the sight of those exposed toes having a bit of a wiggle sparked a strange spear of sensation deep in his gut.

Good grief, he'd been swimming naked with this woman, and she had—albeit by mistake— almost kissed him, and he hadn't felt any inappropriate sexual attraction. But there was something about those bare toes that made him realise, belatedly, the desire he felt for her.

Because he'd just thrown the word 'sex' into the air between them?

Or was it because he knew so much more about Grace now?

Cared more about her?

He had already known how vulnerable Grace was for having been in an abusive relationship. Now he knew that had only been a part of it. He'd already known that she was courageous too, but how far had he underestimated that now that he knew she was so good at helping parents deal with the trauma of miscarriage or stillbirth because she'd been through it herself?

Grace Collins was, quite simply, the most extraordinary woman he'd ever met and, dammit... that water they'd been swimming in was so clear that how perfect her body was hadn't been hidden at all. You'd have to be some sort of saint not to feel a level of physical attraction to her—especially when she was this close to him—with those *bare* feet.

It was just as well she still wasn't looking at him so she couldn't possibly know what he was thinking.

Jock cleared his throat. 'How 'bout I make us something to eat? Have you decided whether you prefer the beans or eggs on toast?'

Grace lifted her head. She was smiling.

'Let's live a little,' she said. 'And have an egg on top of the beans.'

Don't give up on sex...?

And did Jock really think she was special?

The galley was too small for two adults to be in at the same time but Grace was trying to help. She was using a board that went across the tiny sink to cut some toast-sized slices of bread from a loaf while Jock was trying to fit both a frying pan and a small pot on the tiny gas hob.

As long as you don't float away...

Grace had to stop cutting the bread because she needed to close her eyes for a moment.

Denial was real, wasn't it? Had she really believed she wasn't sexually attracted to Jock? Blocked it out because she was so afraid of being that close to someone?

And she had honestly thought that she could only fall in love in a very different time and place?

Well...she'd been wrong, hadn't she?

The realisation was hitting her like a ton of bricks.

She could quite easily fall in love with Jock McKay if she let herself. She wasn't going to let herself, of course, but she couldn't deny that she definitely fancied him...

''Scuse me...'

Grace opened her eyes to find Jock leaning in front of her.

'I just need to get into the drawer to find a can opener for the beans.'

His arm brushed hers but she didn't flinch. She wasn't about to drop what she was holding either. She didn't move a single muscle.

Jock's gaze flicked up to meet hers and Grace knew he was startled by what he could see in her face. Concerned, even?

'Are you okay?' he asked softly. The step back he took felt like it made the boat rock gently.

Grace swallowed. Was she brave enough to say anything? Maybe this newly emerging Grace was…

'I was just thinking about something you said.' She took another breath. 'About not giving up on sex…'

The flash in Jock's eyes revealed more than she'd expected. It also sparked a source of heat deep in her belly that Grace hadn't felt in so long she'd totally forgotten what it was like to feel this…desire, that was what it was.

It was a feeling she'd thought she would never, ever experience again and it was a flicker of something precious. She didn't want to let it go. She wanted…

She wanted to feel more.

To find out if it was even possible to go there

when she'd given up the hope that she'd ever feel like this again.

Jock was watching her—as if he was waiting for her to say more.

'I couldn't do it if I didn't trust someone enough,' Grace said slowly.

'Of course not.'

'As much as I trust you,' she added.

Jock hadn't let go of their eye contact. 'I might not be the man you need, Grace,' he said gently. 'I can't give you what you need in your future. That family and all those kids. A place to call home. I can't be in a place for more than a year without getting itchy feet. And I run a mile if a relationship even looks like getting serious. It's only about the sex.'

'Maybe that's what I need it to be,' Grace whispered. 'Just a one-off kind of experiment. To know if it's possible, even… Or I might not believe that a future with that home and family could ever happen.'

She could see the play of emotion on Jock's face and body language. He was almost nodding, as if he totally agreed with her. As if he thought it was a good idea, even? But he was fighting something—the thought of how horrified Jenni might be probably. Or that it was the last thing he wanted to do?

As *if*…

Grace could feel the colour and heat of embarrassment flooding into her face. 'Sorry,' she said. 'This is a terrible idea. Forget I said anything. Please…'

She dropped the bread knife and would have turned away, but the space was too small and Jock was blocking the exit.

''Scuse me,' she muttered, keeping her head down. 'I need to—'

Escape—that was what she needed to do…

'Hey…'

Jock wasn't moving. He was a solid wall of man in front of Grace. Worse, he put his fingers under her chin and tilted her head so that she had to look up at him.

He wasn't saying anything and the look in his eyes was…

Oh, *my*…

Grace had never been looked at like that by a man in her life. Not even on her wedding night when she was about to lose her virginity. As if she was something rare and precious. As if Jock wanted nothing more than to touch her.

'Are you sure?' he asked, so quietly his words were almost inaudible. 'Would it really help you? To know…?'

Grace hesitated and then gave a single nod, pressing her chin into his hand. 'But that doesn't mean you—'

She didn't get to finish giving him an excuse because Jock bent his head and touched his lips to hers. As softly as he'd just spoken to her. For a long, long moment, that was all it was. The softness. The warmth. The closeness. Movement that almost wasn't there but it still felt like a conversation. Questions being asked and answered.

The odd feeling that her whole body was being supported by the way his fingers were holding her chin.

When she'd burst into tears earlier this evening, it had been as violent as a dam bursting. Now, Grace could feel a softening that was like something uncurling deep inside her. Something growing rather than exploding. A delicious sensation that was a mix of feeling safe but in danger at the same time.

Excitement.

Anticipation.

A heat that was rapidly spreading throughout her body. Grace wanted to sink into it and she made a sound that could have been one of surrender. Her lips moved as she made it, but Jock's mouth followed hers and his hand slipped from her chin to cradle the back of her head instead.

It was the touch—and taste—of his tongue that was the point of no return for Grace. She heard herself make another sound.

One of pure need...?

* * *

Dear *Lord*…

Whatever Jock might have imagined doing as a way of helping Grace overcome the barriers she had to being physically touched, it would never have been this.

It would have been more like encouraging her to date someone else. Someone safe, like Dan, perhaps.

Never in a million years would he have imagined he would be having the most amazing sexual experience in his lifetime.

How could he have imagined something he didn't even know existed in quite this form?

Had the flame of attraction been fanned because this was something they really shouldn't be doing? Okay, they were two single, consenting adults, but Jock had been told in no uncertain terms that he was not to even *think* of doing this to his sister's best friend.

Or was there something completely different at play here?

The fact that he was being invited to try and help heal psychological, physical and emotional damage that had been done to the person who had given him the invitation. That he was being trusted with something that was…huge.

Sex was the only time that Jock allowed himself to feel really close to someone. For such a brief burst of time, he could feel as if the past didn't exist. Or the future. He could live in the present and enjoy the closest human touch it was possible to experience. He could feel as if someone wanted to be with him.

That, even if it was just for a few minutes, he was enough.

It never lasted, of course. He couldn't afford to allow it to. Far safer to move on before he could find out that it was no more than wishful thinking.

But that meant Jock had had a lot of practice at sex and he was confident he was pretty damn good at this. He'd never focused quite like this on the woman in his arms, mind you—reading the body language that the touch of his hands and tongue prompted, hearing every sound she made and the way she was breathing and celebrating every touch that *he* was receiving in return.

Aye...this was like nothing he'd ever had before or ever would again and every moment had to be as good as it possibly could be. Not for him, but for Grace. The fact that it *was* so astonishingly good for him as well was an unexpected bonus.

Jock took the cushions off the narrow beds in the front of the boat and put them on the floor. They were both naked by now and Grace's tumble of blonde hair was loose and wildly tousled as she lay there in front of him. Jock had found a condom in the first aid kit, of all places, but he hesitated for just a moment as he knelt there. He could stop, if he had to.

It might kill him but he could stop.

He leaned down. Holding his body away from hers but getting close enough to give her another lingering kiss.

'Are you sure, sweetheart?' he asked softly. 'Are you sure this is what you want?'

Grace's eyes were so dark they were black. She didn't say anything but the answer to his question couldn't have been any more obvious.

It felt like she was reaching up with her whole body to pull them together so closely he couldn't quite tell where his skin finished and hers began.

There was no need for Jock to find any more words either. He could say everything he needed to with *his* body.

CHAPTER TEN

'I CAN'T *DO* THIS...'

'You are doing it, Jodie. You're nearly there. I think you're close to being fully dilated, which means you'll be able to start pushing soon.'

'I don't *want* to start pushing. I want to go *home*...'

'I know... Moving might help. Let's get you out of the shower. You might like to try leaning against Alec.'

'*No*...' Jodie pushed at her husband's hands as he tried to help her out of the shower in the en suite bathroom of this labour suite. 'Get away from me. I don't want you touching me. You're never going to touch me again. *Ever*...'

Her reference to the conception of this baby made Grace hide a smile as she turned off the shower and draped a soft, dry towel over Jodie's shoulders. It wasn't uncommon for women at this stage of labour to swear they were never going to risk going through this again. The vast majority of them had completely forgotten any such threats of discontinuing their sex life by the time they were holding their babies in their arms.

Even the thought of anybody having—or not having—sex was enough to give Grace a very unfamiliar curl of sensation in her own gut that made that hidden smile even wider. It wasn't enough to be distracting her in any way from her care of Jodie but it was very...pleasant.

No, 'pleasant' was totally the wrong word for the discoveries Grace Collins had made regarding sex last night on Jock's boat. She had always dismissed the heights of passion she'd heard or seen in books and movies as being flights of fantasy that had no basis in reality, but now she knew it could really happen.

She had, miraculously, experienced it for herself and it had quite possibly been...life-changing.

Even if she was only ever going to experience it that one time, she was never going to regret it. And she was certainly never going to forget it because it was always going to make her smile. And give her that oh, so delicious frisson of a sensation that was just the faintest echo of what it felt like to get taken to the edge of paradise and then pushed over it into a space she'd never known existed.

That secret smile vanished a heartbeat later, however, as Grace caught Alec's horrified expression. Was he blaming himself in some way for the ordeal that Jodie was going through now?

'This is transition,' she told him. 'It's not you.'

Jodie was groaning as Grace helped her move. She walked towards the bed and held onto the side, her head down.

'I feel sick,' she said a moment later. And then, 'Maybe I *do* want to push.'

'Let's get you on the bed for a minute then, Jodie. I'd like to check your dilation before giving you the all-clear to start pushing and we can put the CTG on so we can check baby's heart rate during a contraction. You've been in labour for a while now and that's tiring for both of you.'

But Alec was looking a lot happier. 'It won't be long now.' He looked at Grace hopefully. 'Will it?'

'It's Jodie's first time,' Grace reminded him. 'And we know baby's in a slightly tricky position, being face up, but this is when most babies will rotate to get ready for delivery. I'm going to check that as well—if you're okay with another internal examination, Jodie?'

The young woman was climbing wearily onto the bed. 'You do whatever you need to do,' she sighed. 'I just want this baby *out*...'

She was saying exactly the same thing more than an hour later, but now Jodie was sobbing and begging for an epidural anaesthetic she had earlier declared she didn't want.

'I want it *now*,' she pleaded.

'It's a bit more complicated when you're fully

dilated,' Grace told her. 'I'm going to get one of our obstetricians to come and see you, but I need to do a few things first. We need to monitor baby continuously, so you'll need to stay on the bed on your back, but first I need you to go and empty your bladder. If you do get an epidural, you'll have to have a catheter inserted as well.'

'I don't care.'

'Alec, can you go with Jodie while she goes to the loo and help her back to bed, please? Push the button on the wall if you're worried about anything at all in there. I've got a couple of very quick phone calls I need to make.'

'Sure.' The young soon-to-be father was looking as exhausted as his wife.

Grace put out a call to the obstetric team and another one for an anaesthetist, who would be the person to insert the epidural catheter. She also called the ultrasound department to request a portable machine. Jodie's baby had still been in an occipito-posterior position, or face up, when Grace had examined her at the beginning of the second stage of her labour, but now she was facing the possible need for an assisted or surgical delivery and the obstetrician would want to know exactly how the baby was presenting.

Was it unprofessional, she wondered, to be hoping *this* much that it would be Jock who was on his way to help with this delivery?

* * *

'So... I hear you've got a "sunny side up" baby.'

'Like an *egg*?'

Jock nodded solemnly. At least he'd got Jodie's husband, Alec, smiling. How much more anxious would they both be looking if he'd confirmed that their baby had a persistent occipito-posterior presentation and was about to need assistance to be delivered safely.

'Left occipito-posterior.' The ultrasound technician was finishing her urgent examination and this information was important. It would inform the direction of rotation to apply with either a hand or pair of forceps.

'Thanks, Mandy.' Jock perched on the end of Jodie's bed as Mandy moved the portable ultrasound machine, to bring himself to the same level as the young parents. Alec had his arm around Jodie as she lay back against the pillows and she was clinging to his hand with one of her own. Grace was busy securing an IV line she had put into the back of Jodie's other hand. Her head was bent and, with her hair pulled back in a ponytail, he could see the tiny whorls of hair just behind her ear.

Not that Jock was going to allow himself even a nanosecond to remember that he knew exactly how baby-soft that hair was or how delicious the equally soft skin felt and tasted, but it did require an effort.

It was just as well last night had been a 'one-off'. Personal distractions of any kind during working hours were totally unacceptable.

'Here's the thing,' Jock said. 'We were hoping your little one would decide to turn herself around.' He tilted his head to include Grace as part of this team. 'But she's being a wee bit stubborn and we can see that it could become a problem.' Jock picked up the CTG graph that Grace had recorded. 'The way the heart rate is dropping during contractions and taking a while to come back up is a sign that we need to do something. I know you're hoping for an epidural, Jodie, but I think it's too late for that.'

'Oh, *no...*'

'We're going to help you,' Jock added quickly. 'And you're going to see your baby very soon. Worst case scenario is that you'll need a Caesarean and we're going to move you into Theatre to be on the safe side but there are other procedures we can try first, to turn your baby so that she can be born without you needing surgery.'

'Like forceps?' Jodie was sobbing now. 'No... I don't want that... It's not on my plan...'

'Jock needs to do what's safest for you and

baby,' Grace said. 'That's the only thing that matters right now.'

'What would *you* do?'

Jock wasn't surprised that both Alec and Jodie turned to Grace. He could feel the level of trust they had with their midwife.

Grace smiled at them and then turned her head to include Jock in the smile.

'I would trust Jock,' she said quietly. 'Absolutely.'

'What's it like?' Grace was in charge of the toasted sandwich maker in the kitchen as they ate a late meal that evening. 'I mean, I've put pressure on when a baby's crowning to slow down a precipitous birth or get the cord from around the neck. And once I had to keep the head elevated in a cord prolapse while they set up for the C-section, but you were holding the head enough to be able to turn it. That must feel astonishing…'

'Imagine this.' Jock made his hand into a fist and then took Grace's hand to put over it. 'My fist is the baby's head. You need to hold it like this, with your thumb over the right parietal bone, and you put enough pressure on to reduce the foetal head station and push it back far enough to give you the room for rotation, but not too far because that could precipitate a cord prolapse.'

He was pressing Grace's hand gently down on his. 'And then your turn the baby's head. If it's an LOP you use your right hand and turn counter clockwise. If it's ROP you use your left hand and do a clockwise rotation.'

He could feel Grace's hand moving beneath his palm.

'If you meet some resistance, a slight tilt of baby's head towards the chest will help.' He bent Grace's hand a little. 'And when it's turned, you hold it in the anterior position over the next two contractions while you get the mother to push down. That way, you bring the foetal head back down into the pelvic outlet and the occiput under the pubic bone.'

Jock was still holding Grace's hand. Her gaze was fixed on his face.

'And then you've got a natural delivery happening,' she said, 'and a baby with an APGAR score of eight and two parents who think you're the best obstetrician ever.'

Jock could smell the cheese that was bubbling out through the join in the sandwich maker. It was probably time to open the machine and check the bread wasn't getting burnt, but he couldn't take his eyes off Grace and he could see exactly what he was thinking being reflected in her eyes.

'I want to kiss you,' he admitted.

'I want you to,' she said.

Jock bent his head. Grace sucked in a breath.

'We can't,' she whispered.

'Why not?'

'You know why.'

Jock did know why. Because it was highly unlikely it would just be a kiss. There was no reason
not to let his body remember just how incredible
the sex with Grace had been last night and, when
he did, it let him know in no uncertain terms just
how much it would like to repeat the experience.

'It was only supposed to be once.'

'Would it be all that different if it happened to
be twice?' Jock kept his tone deliberately casual.
'I mean, it was supposed to be an experiment,
wasn't it?'

'Mmm…' Grace was staring at his mouth.

'And it worked…?' He was trying not to sound
smug now.

'Mmm…'

'Most scientists would say that the experiment
would have to be repeated, just to check that the
first results were trustworthy.'

Grace had closed her eyes. Because she didn't
want him to know what she was thinking? Did
she realise she was leaning into him—as if being
drawn closer by a magnetic force? He dipped his
head a little more. Far enough for his lips to be
almost brushing hers.

'What's the real reason not to? Because we agreed we don't want Jenni to know anything about this?'

'She was right. It would be too weird. It might mess with our friendship.'

'And I'd feel guilty,' Jock admitted. 'Not that I made a promise that I wouldn't lay a finger on you. She just assumed I did.'

'She'd know.' Grace was decisive. 'And it might spoil her visit.'

'Not if it had stopped happening before she got here.'

'That's only a couple of weeks away.'

'More than enough time to make sure the experiment really was a success.' Jock let his lips settle on hers for just a heartbeat. It wasn't as if he was a stranger to intense but deliberately short physical relationships. 'A "use-by" date like that is perfect,' he murmured. 'By the time she gets here we can be absolutely telling the truth when we say we're just good friends. She's not going to ask too many questions, anyway. We do know when to respect each other's privacy.'

Jock reached past Grace to turn the sandwich maker off.

He didn't want the house to start burning down while he kissed her as thoroughly as he intended to.

* * *

It was a risk, of course.

The bar had been set so high the first time that Grace wasn't at all sure the sex could be anything like as good as that again. She was risking that memory, in fact. The memory she had spent today thinking she could rely on if she ever needed to feel better about herself. *Special*... Or just to feel better about the world in general. Or dream of a future, perhaps, where she wouldn't be alone.

But Jock was right. If she really was going to give that future another chance and not give up on finding a partner, then making sure that experiment had really broken through those barriers could only help.

What if the sex on the boat had only been that amazing because it was a result of not only an over-emotional day at work but the result of that dam bursting in the wake of telling Jock why it had affected her on such a personal level? A fantasy that had begun when she had accepted that she was attracted to him. That she could imagine falling in love with him, even.

It would be different this time. Her feet were back on the ground. She wasn't about to let herself fall in love with Jock McKay because the last thing she wanted was to get her heart broken. She did, however, want to have sex with him again. What woman wouldn't?

It wasn't as if she was initiating it this time either. Jock wanted this.

He wanted *her,* and that was enough to make Grace feel a little giddy.

And it *was* different. *Better…*

Because they were already more familiar with each other's bodies and Grace was learning that it was possible to relax—have *fun* in bed, even—and still feel safe. This had a 'use-by' date, after all.

Even if Jenni wasn't on her way to visit them, it would have only ever been a temporary thing. Jock never stayed in one place—or with one person—long enough for it to be anything else.

Knowing that so clearly up front meant that no one was going to get hurt here.

So maybe they should just make the most of it.

There was nothing like a ticking clock to provide focus.

Mixing in the fantasy of something that was a big step away from reality in that it wasn't a *real* relationship only increased every aspect of it—like a brief holiday on a tropical island, perhaps.

Or an intensely passionate relationship with what should have been a completely unsuitable, unavailable man.

It wasn't just the sex, despite that being the

most obvious fantastical part of what was going on for Grace.

No…whatever was happening between them physically was permeating every minute of every day in the countdown to when Jock was going to drive down to Christchurch to collect Jenni from her international flight coming in from Glasgow via London and Singapore. It was there in that first sip of coffee in the morning, when she could catch Jock's gaze over the rim of her mug, and it was there last thing at night, when they had that silent conversation that could happen in a single glance.

Are you tired?
Not that tired.
Do you want to…?
Yes…oh, yes, I do…

It was there constantly at work.

If they were both involved in the same case, if felt as if there was almost an extra dimension to the passion Grace brought to her work—because she wanted Jock to be impressed with her—the way he had been when she'd been with Yvonne and David through the trauma of losing their baby.

When they *weren't* working together, there was that delicious possibility of just seeing him coming towards her down a corridor or in the café and feeling the hum of that secret between them. Perhaps it was there especially when they were not working together, with a mother and her baby that required their complete focus, because that was when she could let herself sink into that…what was it…the warmth of gratitude? Excitement? Or was it as simple as pure happiness?

Whatever it was, it felt like it was powerful enough to be spreading.

An antenatal clinic gave Grace the chance to catch up with Maureen, who was happily nesting as she got further into her final trimester and wanted to share pictures of the nursery furniture she'd ordered online that included the latest trend of a bedside crib with a detachable bassinet.

'Look, it's got see-through mesh windows and a zip-down wall. I won't even have to get out of bed to do night feeds.'

'And it gives baby a safe sleeping space instead of bed sharing,' Grace noted. 'It's a brilliant idea.'

Stella looked even happier when she came in later, having just had her anatomy scan ultrasound.

'It's a girl,' she told Grace as she lay on the bed to get her fundal height measured. 'I would have been just as happy to have another boy, as long as he was healthy, but Scott has set his heart on having a little sister to look after and I think his dad had his fingers crossed too, judging by his reaction to the picture I sent him of a pair of pink booties.'

'What did he say?' Grace turned the tape measure to eliminate any bias by being able to see the number of centimetres. With one hand, she secured the end on the point where she palpated the top of the fundus to be.

'It was a whole shower of love hearts.'

'Nice.' Grace kept the tape in contact with Stella's skin as she smoothed it down towards the symphysis pubis where the left and right sides of the lower pelvis met in the centre. 'Does Scott know yet?'

'No. I'm trying to think of a way we could do a kind of private gender reveal. Just for him.'

'Hmm…' Grace thought about that as she recorded the measurement she had just taken. 'You're nearly seventeen centimetres, Stella. Right on track.'

'The ultrasound technician, Mandy, said she'd be sending the results through to Dr McKay but it didn't matter that my appointment wasn't until next week. She said everything looks great.' Stella was smiling again. 'And she said that you don't often get such a clear view of gender at this stage but she's a hundred percent sure that it's a girl.'

'I'd love to see Scott's face when he finds out he's got a baby sister on the way.'

'He'll be more excited than he was for his own birthday celebrations.'

'There's an idea. You could get a birthday balloon and put pink glitter inside it for Scott to pop? Or buy a real pair of pink booties and leave them somewhere for him to find? Or have a pass the parcel game with something pink wrapped up in the centre?'

'I love that idea. We might keep it a secret just for a bit longer. It's kind of special having a grown-up secret that's just for the two of you, isn't it?'

'Oh, yes...' Grace's agreement was whole-hearted. She knew exactly how special it was.

She got to share Stella's news with Jock later that day and a few days later she got to tell him all about her home visit to Jodie and her baby.

'She and Alec are sleep deprived and anxious like all first-time parents, of course, but they're doing so well,' she said. 'And they're just *so* happy that everything went as well as it did at the end. They wanted me to thank you again for that.'

The smile they shared encompassed everything Grace loved about this job that she had chosen to do for the rest of her life—the joy, the tension, the drama and even panic that could be part of the miracle of bringing new lives into the world and the incredible satisfaction of beating the odds sometimes to create and share a very happy ending. Sharing it with someone she was coming to know on a very intimate level brought an entirely different dimension to every aspect of it.

Life had never been this good, in fact, and that ticking clock was making it a no-brainer to enjoy it while it lasted and not worry about any consequences. They both knew this was temporary.

Like a holiday fling on that tropical island.

And yes, they might miss it when it was over, but knowing that was coming mitigated any effects that might seriously disrupt their lives, didn't it? Jock seemed to think so and he had way more experience in playing this particular game, so Grace was perfectly happy to follow his lead.

She had the excitement of a visit from her best friend to look forward to as well.

A visit that would, hopefully, provide an easy step from fantasy back into reality.

CHAPTER ELEVEN

'I STILL CAN'T believe how different you look.'

Every time Grace had looked up since Jenni had arrived she'd found her friend staring at her. And smiling—as if Grace was radiating a contagious sort of happiness. A leftover dollop of that *joie de vivre* she'd been spreading at work in the last couple of weeks, perhaps?

'If I didn't know better,' Jenni said, shaking her head, 'I'd swear that you were madly in love with someone.'

If Grace was slightly overdoing the laughter intended to make it seem like something ridiculous had been suggested, she could at least blame it on the wine-tasting they were having in the gorgeous Tuscan-styled buildings of one of the most popular local vineyards, but she'd seen the way Jock suddenly froze with a wine glass from the middle of the array in front of him poised in mid-air.

Did he think that Jenni was picking up on something that they'd both been confident was safely buried by now? Or worse, that there might have been more going on than he would be re-motely comfortable with? Jock didn't do 'falling in love' himself and it was obvious he backed off at any hint of it happening in what was supposed to be a casual relationship. How appalled would he be if he thought she'd been reading too much into what had happened between them?

'You know me better than that, Jen,' Grace said firmly. 'I'm still happily single, thank you. Maybe I'm just in love with my new life in New Zealand. Who wouldn't be, with this sort of treat on your doorstep?' She lifted the wine glass that contained the small sample of the vineyard's new rosé, but she was the designated driver today so she barely tasted it.

'That's true,' Jenni conceded. 'And we get a girls' day out tomorrow with our ferry ride and shopping trip to Wellington. Are you sure you don't want to change your mind and come with us, Jock?'

'I'm working. And I'm sure you two need some time to yourselves.' Jock finished the taste of the wine he was holding. 'I'm going to buy some of this Pinot Gris while we're here. Like drinking velvet, it is.'

His smile was the same as it had been the day Grace had arrived in New Zealand. Cheeky and warm and totally genuine. Only she could know that he was reminding her of the night they went skinny-dipping.

The night they'd made love for the first time.

Maybe he was also saluting the last time. And letting her know that he appreciated how easy she was making their transition back to being simply friends? How relieved he was that she wasn't giving it any major significance?

By mutual agreement, the experiment to see if Grace wanted to revive her sex life had been declared complete several days before Jenni had even been due to arrive in the country. It had been a complete success, it was probably well past its 'use-by' date and they could both move on with no regrets. Their new mission was to ensure that Jenni didn't guess they had strayed past the boundaries of being the good friends they would hopefully be for the rest of their lives.

Jock had given the impression that the plan was working perfectly when he'd arrived back from his trip to collect Jenni from the airport in Christchurch. They had stayed a night in Kaikōura on the way back, eaten crayfish, visited the fur seal colony to watch the babies playing in the nursery on the rocks below the main road and had been lucky enough to spot both sperm and orca whales on a boat tour. Jenni had borrowed Grace's car and gone exploring on her own when Jock and Grace were working. They were doing a tour of vineyards around the Marlborough district and tomorrow, while Jock was working, Grace was taking Jenni on the ferry over to Wellington for a day trip.

'You certainly look happier than I've ever seen you look.' Jenni was still focused on Grace. 'But I can understand why. I'm loving it here. Maybe *I* should come back to New Zealand on a more permanent basis.'

'Now *that's* a brilliant idea,' Jock said.

'We're still short-staffed.' Grace nodded. 'I'm sure you could get a job here as easily as I did. And start as soon as you wanted to.' She caught her breath, catching another shaft of that recent happiness that she'd known was too good to be true because it wasn't real. 'It would be *so* good to have you here, Jen.'

'I might actually think about it,' Jenni mused. 'I could get used to all this sunshine and the food and wine. And cooking dinner on the barbecue every night. That's something that's a rare treat in Glasgow.'

'That reminds me,' Jock said. 'I've made a booking at a Brazilian restaurant for your last night here. Then you'll know how good barbecue can really be. It's the most popular place in town—apart from the new cocktail bar that just opened near the Fisherman's Reserve. Maybe we'll go there as well and make the night one to remember.'

'A party!' Jenni grinned. 'I like that idea.'

'You'll probably meet some of the people you'd be working with if you moved here,' Grace said. 'That might help persuade you to take the plunge.'

'That's true,' Jock agreed. 'Shall we invite some people to join us, just to make sure it happens? Like Dan?'

'Who's Dan?' Jenni asked.

'An anaesthetist at the hospital. He's Jock's fishing buddy,' Grace told her. 'I think Jock entertained the idea of setting me up with him when I first arrived. And no...' she shook her head at Jenni's raised eyebrows '... I haven't been out with him. He wasn't any more interested than I was. I got the impression that he's just as much of a committed bachelor as Jock is.'

'No harm in you and this Dan getting to know each other better,' Jenni decreed. 'And Jock, maybe you could bring whoever it is you're seeing at the moment. Is that someone who works at the hospital too? Or is it still that gorgeous Swedish girl...what was her name?'

'Greta.' Jock shook his head. 'No, that was over a while ago.' He seemed to be avoiding looking at Grace. 'Have you tried this sparkling wine, Jen? It's really good.'

But Jenni wasn't going to be distracted.

'There must be someone new,' she said. 'You never stay single for long. Invite her. And find me a date for the night so I don't feel like a fifth wheel at my own party.'

'Fine…' Jock threw her a smile. 'I'll see who's around.' He glanced at his watch. 'We should get going. We don't want to be late home when you two have got an early start to catch the ferry to-morrow.'

It was a perfect morning.

Dawn was breaking as the inter-island ferry sailed through the Sounds towards the short space of open sea that would take them into the pictur-esque harbour of the country's capital city.

Grace and Jenni were at the back of the ship, leaning over the rail, soaking in the spectacular scenery.

'This is unbelievably beautiful,' Jenni sighed.

'I did this trip when I first arrived, sailing in from Wellington to Picton, and it felt like I was coming home,' Grace told her.

'No wonder you look so happy.'

'You could always come and live here just for a while,' Grace suggested. 'It doesn't have to be for ever. Why not put in an application form just in case? It can take up to a couple of months for applications to be processed, but then you can get a work permit and just have it ready.'

'I'll think about it,' Jenni agreed. 'But it would have to be just a long holiday. Scotland's home. I'd never want to live anywhere else for too long. Maybe I'm scared that I'll end up like Jock and never stop long enough to put down roots and feel like it *is* a real home.'

'Do you think that's why Jock keeps moving? Because he doesn't want to get attached to a place?' Grace pulled in a breath. 'Or a person? Has it come from that vow you both made to never get married or have kids?'

'Jock told you about that?' Jenni sounded surprised.

'He said it was because you got caught up in your mother going from one disaster to the next.'

'She thought that finding someone to love her would be the answer to all her problems. Apart from the ones she couldn't get rid of—the kids she'd never wanted. Somehow it was always our fault when things didn't work out.' Jenni let her breath out in a sigh. 'Maybe *she* should have gone looking for a place instead of a person. I want roots that I can trust are strong enough to hold me in one place. What we didn't have when we were kids. I think Jock's problem is that he doesn't realise that's what he's searching for too. Maybe *he* should come back to Scotland. I'd hate to think he's going to end up feeling lost. Or lonely.'

Grace opened her mouth with the intention of

confessing that she had worried about exactly the same thing. That she liked Jock enough to know he didn't deserve to be lonely. She wanted to admit that they'd broken the rules and got so much closer than Jenni had thought they should, but she didn't have enough time to find the words she needed because Jenni was talking again.

'Home's the place where you feel properly safe, you know?' She shook her head. 'Of course you know. It's because you needed to feel safe that you've come twelve thousand miles to get away from your ex and start a new life.' She threw her arms around Grace and hugged her. 'And you've done that and I love that you feel at home here. That you're so happy. I'm proud of you.'

Grace let go of her intention to confess. She wasn't going to spoil this day with her best friend by telling Jenni something that could not only change their friendship but make things awkward between Jenni and her twin when they only had a small amount of time left to enjoy each other's company.

Instead, she just hugged Jenni back. 'You know that quote about today being the first day of the rest of your life?'

'The one that gets written on an inspirational picture like the view we're looking at right now?'

'Exactly… We're inside that picture. This really is the first day of the rest of our lives.'

Except that wasn't quite true for Grace, was it? The real first day of the rest of her life had been the day that Jock had reached behind her barriers and given her his hand to lead her out.

The day he'd made love to her.

'All we need now is for some dolphins to swim past,' she added, laughing.

'And to have the best day ever together. What's first when we get to Wellington?'

'We're going to take a cable car up the hill to get the best view of the city and harbour. We can visit the museum, have lunch on the waterfront somewhere, and I've been told that the best place to go shopping is in Cuba Street. We can find new dresses to wear for your farewell party tomorrow night. Oh, and we have to get a photo taken in front of the Bucket Fountain. I have no idea what that is, but it's apparently quite famous.'

How good was this?

If he'd wanted to make absolutely sure that Jenni ended the best time together they'd had in years without it being spoilt by her finding out that he'd broken the rules she'd made regarding Grace, this was the ace he hadn't known he had up his sleeve.

Inviting a few friends and colleagues to make it a really good night out had been a masterstroke. It was Saturday night, the Brazilian restaurant had a live band playing salsa music and there was great conversation and a lot of laughter and Jenni thought—as he'd intended her to—that he'd invited Mandy, the ultrasound technician, as his date. Maybe she was looking to see if she could detect any spark between Grace and Dan—who had reluctantly agreed to join this social gathering—and she was enjoying the company of Stefano, the Italian ED locum doctor who Jock had invited to keep the numbers even.

Stefano was certainly enjoying himself. He had taken charge of a platter that was part of the entrees they were all sharing. Jenni and Mandy had already taken some and he was passing it to Grace now. 'You have to try these cheese bread balls,' he told her. 'They are *così delizioso*.' He kissed his fingers like a chef. 'So delicious.'

'They are,' Mandy confirmed, smiling at Stefano. 'Can I have another one, please?'

Grace also took one and bit into it. 'Oh…you're right. How good is that? Oops…messy…' She caught the drips of melted cheese on her fingers with her tongue.

Jock knew he shouldn't be staring but, for a fraction too long, he couldn't look away. Both Jenni and Grace were wearing the new dresses they'd bought on their shopping spree in Wellington yesterday and they both looked gorgeous, but the dark blue of Grace's dress matched her eye colour and she had left her hair loose so that it fell in bouncy golden waves to her shoulders.

She was looking absolutely stunning.

And she was licking melted cheese off her fingers, dammit...

Thanks to the twist of sensation in his gut, all Jock could think of was having to turn off that sandwich maker while it was cooking cheese toasties so that he could make love to Grace without burning the house down. His entire body was reminding him of how much he'd wanted her that night.

How much he *still* wanted her, even though they had agreed that the experiment was complete and it had been a success. Jock had achieved exactly what he'd wanted and had helped Grace get past the barriers that were keeping her from living her best life and achieving her dream future of a family of her own.

He should be happy about that. So why wasn't he?

Why did he have this odd empty feeling he couldn't quite place? And why wasn't he remotely attracted to Mandy, who was supposed to be his date tonight?

Not that it mattered. Everyone was enjoying themselves as the evening went on. Mandy seemed to be getting on very well with Stefano as they all shared and enjoyed their main dishes of barbecued fish and spicy chicken and a smoky black bean stew with rice. Jock and Dan started planning their next fishing expedition and Jenni and Grace were clearly making the most of their remaining time with each other. Grace was going to miss her friend after tomorrow, wasn't she?

And that was when it hit him.

That was what that hollow feeling in his gut was about. Jock was missing Grace, even though she was right here, sitting across the table from him.

He'd been missing her for days. Ever since they'd declared the experiment over and done with before Jenni had arrived in town. Ever since he'd had to be careful not to let his gaze rest on Grace for too long or share a smile that might advertise a connection that had been far more intimate than merely friendship.

While the dishes were being cleared from the table the band started up again after a break and Stefano looked hopefully at the women around him.

'So…who wants to do some salsa dancing?'

'Me…' Mandy said, as both Jenni and Grace shook their heads.

Stefano held out his hand and within seconds they were both on the small floor area right in front of the band. They were both good dancers and their body language made it clear that they

were increasingly enjoying each other's company.
Inviting Stefano to be Jenni's date tonight had
clearly backfired as much as pretending he was
out on a date with Mandy, but when Jock offered
his sister an apologetic grimace, Jenni just smiled.

'You win some, you lose some,' she said. 'I
won't be offended if you're not.'

'We're not going to let it spoil the party,' Grace
said. 'Do you want to order dessert or is it time to
go and check out that cocktail bar?'

'Let's give them five minutes more dancing and
then go and get cocktails.' Jenni turned back to
Dan. 'So how long did you say you've been living here?'

'Couple of years now.'

'What made you choose Picton?'

'Job came up. I needed a change.'

Jock hid a smile. He'd asked the same question
himself and got exactly the same answer. Dan
might be taciturn but he was consistent. Trustworthy. It was a shame there was no spark there between him and Grace. She wasn't even joining in
the conversation at the moment because she was
watching Mandy and Stefano dancing together.
As if she felt Jock's gaze, however, Grace turned
and there was no mistaking the invitation that lit
up her eyes. She wanted to dance too.

It was more than an invitation. Maybe it was

more than simply wanting to dance. It looked like…longing…

He could feel it himself. He wanted to hold Grace in his arms and feel her body close to his own. He wanted it so much, in fact, that he knew how dangerous it would be to respond to that invitation.

Worse…he didn't care. He wanted to respond. He needed to…?

Maybe it was fortunate that his phone rang to break the moment.

'Sorry… I'll have to get that. I'm second on call.' Jock got up from the table to take the call from the hospital, but he came back a short time later.

'I have to go in,' he said. 'We've got a seven months' pregnant woman who's come in via ambulance after a car accident. She's at risk of a placental abruption.'

'Someone local?' Grace was getting to her feet.

'Yes.' Jock lowered his voice. 'A Maureen Petersen—do you know her?'

'She's one of *my* mums.' Grace looked horrified. 'I should come with you.' She bit her lip, turning back to Jenni. 'This is important,' she said quietly. 'I know how much this pregnancy means to her.'

'Go,' Jenni said instantly. 'Don't worry about me. We can catch up later at the cocktail bar.'

'It might take a while,' Jock warned.

'I can find my way home in that case. I'll see you both tomorrow morning, anyway, before I get the train back to Christchurch.'

'Sorry, Jen.'

Jock *was* sorry to leave his sister on the last night of her visit but he couldn't stay. He couldn't suggest that Grace stayed either. He could see exactly how worried she was for Maureen. She looked like she had that day she'd followed Stella when she'd run away from that first antenatal appointment. And that time when she'd been such a part of the shared grief for that tiny still-born baby, Luna. Grace cared deeply about every mother and baby she had in her care and he couldn't leave her here, not knowing what was happening.

Because he cared about *her* as well.

Dan must have picked up on the dilemma. 'Don't worry,' he said. 'I'll look after Jenni. Go. You're needed—both of you.'

CHAPTER TWELVE

'GRACE... I'M *SO* glad you're here. But how did you know I'd had an accident?'

'I was just lucky to be in the right place at the right time, Maureen.'

With Jock...

Grace had a feeling that being with Jock might always feel like she was in the right place at the right time. She had thrown a gown over her dress as they'd arrived in Picton Hospital's emergency department and then followed Jock straight to the resuscitation area, where Maureen was lying on the bed, clearly distraught.

She could hear Jock talking to the consultant on duty in Emergency behind her as a technician was positioning an ultrasound machine near the head of the bed.

'Is the speed of the vehicle known?'

'Ambulance crew said it was a low impact, single vehicle crash but the driver's front airbag deployed for some reason. There's a mild abrasion on her face.'

'Was she wearing a seatbelt?'

'Yes. And there's a mark on her shoulder but the belly's clear.'

'Any PV blood loss?'

'No.'

'Abdo pain?'

'Yes. She's complaining of abdominal discomfort.'

Maureen was terrified. 'Something like this can start labour, can't it?' she asked Grace, her voice shaking. 'Or make the placenta come away?'

'You're not bleeding,' Grace said. 'That's a good sign. Jock's going to have a look with the ultrasound now. He'll be able to see if there's any injury to the baby or hidden bleeding from any damage to the placenta. It doesn't sound like you were going very fast.'

'I wasn't. I was getting home after being out for dinner. My shoe slipped on the brake and I hit the accelerator by mistake. I drove straight into my brick fence.' Maureen pressed her hands to her face. 'I can't *believe* this has happened...'

'Hi, Maureen.' Jock was by the bedside now. He touched her arm in a gesture of both greeting and an understanding of how frightened she was. 'Take a deep breath for me, hold Grace's hand and try and slow your breathing down a little if you can. We'll see if we can find out exactly what's going on. Can I have a feel of your tummy before we do the ultrasound? Is it still sore?'

'It just feels…weird. Kind of tight.'

'Have you felt baby moving since the accident?'

'No…' Maureen was crying again. 'I've been so careful when I'm driving ever since I got pregnant. I knew to put my seat back and tilt the steering wheel up. I make sure I put the lap belt under my bump and the other one between my breasts.'

'This'll be a bit cold.' Jock squeezed gel onto Maureen's belly as he finished palpating her abdomen. He picked up the transducer and within seconds they could all hear the reassuring sound of the baby's steady, rapid heartbeat.

'There you go…' Grace squeezed Maureen's hand. 'That's exactly what we want to hear.'

Jock was focused on the screen and Grace watched as he had a quick look for anything major happening to the placenta, which was the main risk to Maureen's baby at present. Then he examined the unborn baby from head to toe for any visible injuries like fractured bones. She could feel the tension in Maureen's body. Maybe that was contributing to why her abdomen felt so tight?

'Deep breath,' she whispered. 'I know it's hard, but it's better for both you and baby if you can relax a little.' Maureen's own heart rate was too fast and her breathing still rapid and shallow, which was pushing her blood pressure higher than normal.

'But what if I go into labour? It's too soon.'

'There's nothing to suggest you will go into labour yet,' Grace said. 'But you're almost thirty weeks. Ninety-eight percent of babies born at thirty weeks survive.'

'Really?'

Grace smiled as she nodded but she gave Maureen's hand another squeeze. She totally understood how stressful this was. She could remember all too well what it was like to be wanting her baby to be safe and healthy. To be looking forward so much to its birth.

She could feel it so strongly, in fact, that it was doing something strange to her own body. Or her heart?

Something almost shocking was happening to her. Something that, only a matter of weeks ago, Grace would never have believed could ever happen again. She was feeling the longing to have a baby of her own tucked into her belly, beneath her heart. To be dreaming of what life would be like when it was born and her life changed for ever because she was a mother. She could *feel* the love she would have for that baby and child.

Jock was smiling at Maureen now. 'There's no sign of any injury to your baby,' he said. 'I'm just going to have a really good look at the placenta now, okay?'

Maureen just nodded, too emotional to speak. They both watched as he located the placenta.

'I'm looking for even a tiny tear now, where it could be coming away from the uterine wall,' he explained. 'And any blood that might be hiding between the placenta and the wall, which would mean it wasn't visible as external loss and... I can't see anything.' He smiled again. 'So far, so good, but we're going to monitor you for a while. Grace will put on the CTG machine and that way we'll know if you start getting any contractions and we'll also be able to listen to the heart rate continuously.'

Maureen nodded again. 'How long for?'

'At least six hours,' Jock said. 'But we're not going to send you home until we're quite sure nothing's going to happen.'

'But what if it does?' Maureen looked as if she was holding her breath.

'Then we'll manage it,' Jock said calmly. 'If there's a risk that you're going into premature labour, we can try and slow things down and give you medications to help the baby's lung development. If we can't stop it or there's any danger to the baby and it's going to be safer to be born, then we'll manage that too.'

'I'll stay with you,' Grace added. She caught

Maureen's gaze as she wiped the gel off her skin. 'We've got this…'

The words were as much for herself as for Maureen. Her own emotional reaction to this situation was something to put aside and think about later.

Maureen's return smile was wobbly but it was there. She saw her gaze slide sideways to watch Jock as he was scribbling notes on her chart and Grace could see her finally trying to slow her breathing as Jock had advised. She was beginning to let go of at least some of her fear.

Grace could understand why. Jock had an amazing ability to demonstrate a combination of confidence and caring that would make anybody trust him completely, even with something as precious as a longed-for baby. She had seen it time and again now, with Stella and Jodie and Tessa amongst others.

She was proud of him for being so good at his job.

Grace wanted him to be proud of the way she did her job too. She placed the flat, round transducers of the cardiotocography machine on Maureen's belly, one above the foetal heart to monitor the rate and stability of the baby's heartbeat and another one at the top of the uterus to pick up any contractions that might be happening, including light ones like Braxton Hicks, explaining what she was doing and making Maureen as comfortable as possible.

When she took another set of vital signs, Maureen's heart rate and breathing were slower and she was smiling as she listened to the steady tick of her baby's heart.

'I could listen to that all night,' she said.

'That's probably just what we will be doing,' Grace said. 'But I'm hoping you'll get some sleep as well.'

'That sounds like a good plan.' Jock looked over Grace's shoulder as she wrote down her vital sign recordings. 'Try and rest, Maureen. I imagine they'll move you somewhere a bit quieter than in here, but you'll be quite safe with Grace here looking after you and I'll be hanging around for a while myself.'

Grace turned her head just enough to catch his gaze and they shared a smile. She turned back to hang the chart on the end of the bed, but she was thinking that it was Jock's care as much as the comfort of hearing the baby's heartbeat that was helping Maureen feel so much calmer. The smile on her face as she listened to Jock suggested that she knew how lucky she was to have him as her obstetrician.

Grace was even luckier because she knew was it was like to have this man as a friend. She knew what it felt like to have given this man a level of trust that she knew had changed her life for the better. A level of trust that was a form of love.

Yeah… The more she got to know Jock, the more she was coming to love him.

She loved who he was as a person and as a friend as much as how skilled and compassionate he was as a doctor.

Grace could feel herself relaxing and, as she mirrored Maureen by taking a deep breath herself and letting it out slowly, she gradually became aware of something else.

Something huge that must have been hiding in plain sight all along.

Something as shocking as realising that she could—*did?*—still want to have her own baby.

The love she was feeling for Jock wasn't simply the result of a close friendship. She was *in* love with him.

Oh, dear Lord…

When had that happened?

That night she'd overreacted to the touch of his hand on her shoulder and had smashed that plate on the kitchen floor? When he'd told her that she would always be safe with him?

Or was it when he'd apparently broken through the tangled self-protective barriers that had been holding her bound too tightly to be properly alive—when he'd offered to push her off the boat?

When he'd held her in his arms to let her cry…

No… Grace suspected it had been when he'd been floating beside her in that icy, clear water. Holding her hand like an otter, so that she wouldn't float away…

Not that it mattered.

It had happened. And it was never going to change.

Grace was in love with Jock.

And it wasn't just *a* baby she could feel herself longing for.

It was *Jock's* baby.

CHAPTER THIRTEEN

THERE WAS SOMETHING different about Grace to-night.

Was it because this was the first time they'd both responded to an after-hours call and gone into the hospital at this time of night?

Was it because he knew she had a pretty new dress on underneath that gown?

Or was it a remnant of how he'd been feeling earlier this evening—that disturbing awareness of how much he'd wanted to dance with Grace? The feeling that he was missing her even though she was right there…

While Grace went with Maureen as they shifted her into a quiet room on the maternity ward to monitor her for at least the rest of the night, Jock went to find a coffee and send Jenni a text.

Will be here for a while yet. You okay?

A response pinged back quickly. It was a pho-tograph of a very fancy-looking cocktail in a martini glass that had a rim crusted with sugar or salt and tiny flowers floating on the top. Another one came in a moment later, of Dan looking as though the last thing he wanted was to have his photograph taken, and was followed by a happy face emoji.

Jock sent back a 'thumbs up' one.

I'll try not to wake you up when I get home. See you in the morning in time to get to the train station. Have fun.

And then he sent another one with a winking face.

Not too much fun...

He couldn't blame his sister for not responding to that one, but in the time he stared at the blank screen Jock found himself thinking about Grace.

Or, rather, he was *seeing* her—as clearly as if she was in the same space he was in.

Seeing the way she'd been looking at him earlier tonight, when it seemed obvious she was hoping he'd ask her to dance with him.

Seeing the way she'd smiled at him when they'd both been offering Maureen their care and reassurance. The kind of smile that acknowledged their shared professional anxiety for the woman who was so afraid of losing what could be her only chance of becoming a mother and their joint determination to keep both mother and baby safe.

But had there been more to that smile? Something far more personal?

Aye…that was it. There *had* been something different about that smile. Or the look in Grace's eyes. Or the alchemy of the combination.

Something that had touched Jock somewhere very deep in his chest.

In his heart…?

Oh…*help*…

Alarm bells were sounding in his head now. Loudly enough to suggest that he'd missed a chance to hear them much earlier than this.

What was even more disturbing was that he knew why those alarms had been set in the first place and what they were about.

He'd learned long ago to recognise the warning signs of getting in too deep in a relationship. The pull to get close to a particular woman, even if it was purely sexual, was a huge red flag. This was new territory because it went above and beyond anything as simple as physical desire and it was alarming because it was even further along a relationship spectrum. That hollow feeling in his gut that was the emptiness of missing something—or some*one*—important in his life was deeper now. Darker. He could fall into it if he didn't do something to protect himself.

That smile, that look, the whole *softness* about Grace in that moment, had offered him something he couldn't allow himself to even consider accepting because it would be unbearable if it was taken away. Possibly unsurvivable.

Love...

Jock was an expert in sensing the exact moment when it was time to move on in any kind of relationship, but it felt like something had gone very wrong this time.

Had he been lulled into a sense of false security because there had been a very definite 'use-by' date on the experiment? Or because, thanks to those ground rules Jenni had put in place, they'd both felt safe with each other from the moment Grace had arrived in his life?

Jock didn't feel safe now.

An unpleasant flicker of something menacing made Jock feel as if he was in danger.

No...he *knew* he was in danger.

In danger of falling in love with Grace Collins.

But maybe it wasn't too late. At least he could hear the alarm sounding now.

And if he stayed in control and moved fast enough, perhaps he could escape unscathed.

How he could manage that escape without people getting hurt in the process was another matter entirely, but at least he didn't have to think about it just yet.

Right now, he could focus on the patient he'd been called in to see this evening. And then he'd have to catch enough sleep to be able to do his job safely tomorrow, and he wanted to farewell Jenni and get her on the train in the morning to reach her flight to Australia in time without giving her any hint of undercurrents—real or threatened—due to the connection he had inadvertently allowed to go too far with Grace.

Yes…there was every reason to put off thinking about it at all until he had a safe time and space. And who knew? Maybe the universe would offer up a solution in the meantime.

It wasn't the universe that unexpectedly offered up the solution the next day. It was Jenni.

Jock was taking one last look around the station platform before his sister climbed into the train carriage. And frowning.

'Looks like Grace isn't going to get away from the hospital in time to wave you off.'

'She texted me. Her patient is getting a bit wound up about the next ultrasound she's waiting for. I told her not to worry. I'll call her when I've arrived in Melbourne. I've had the loveliest time, Jock.' Jenni threw her arms around her brother and hugged him. Hard. 'And thank you… You're doing a great job of looking after Grace. I'm so happy that *she's* so happy.'

'Me too,' Jock managed. 'You look after yourself, Jen. Have fun in Melbourne.'

'I intend to. Have you ever been?'

'No. I'd love to, though.'

And there it was… The solution.

It was time to move on to a new adventure. A new start. He could get away from any danger of things getting out of control with Grace and either of them getting hurt and he knew he could do it in a way that was kind—he was just doing what he always did, after all, and he was confident that he was good at it.

He was moving on.

Hopefully without leaving any lasting damage to what felt like the most significant friendship he'd ever had. Jock was, without doubt, closer to Grace Collins than he'd ever been to anyone other than his twin sister.

The sister who was delighted with how happy Grace was in her new life and the part Jock had been playing in looking after her best friend.

He just had to continue doing that. And it wouldn't hurt to keep his fingers crossed and hope the next step would be as easy to find as the first.

It was easy to put the issue aside when he arrived at work, especially as Grace was with the first patient he needed to see. Being in the dim light of the ultrasound room made it easy to focus completely on the screen and the relief of being able to confirm there was no sign of any damage to Maureen's baby or the placenta made it a good start to his day.

'The continuous CTG monitoring hasn't given us any grounds for concern either, Maureen,' he said. 'I'm happy to discharge you to go home, but it would be a good idea to take things easy for a day or two.'

'And call us if you're worried about anything at all,' Grace added.

He spotted Grace a short time later, on his way to get a sandwich and coffee from the café for lunch. She was walking with Maureen out of the main doors of the hospital to where a taxi was waiting. He bought an extra sandwich and presented it to Grace as she came back through the reception area.

'Ham salad on sourdough,' he said. 'I thought you might need some sustenance. You must be exhausted after being up all night with Maureen.'

'Thank you…' Grace's face looked pale but her smile reached all the way to her eyes. 'I am tired but I'm okay. And so happy that Maureen's baby is also okay. Was Jenni upset that I didn't make it to the train station?'

'Not at all. She's looking forward to telling you all about Melbourne later.'

'She loved being here, didn't she?'

'She did.'

'She'll love Melbourne too. I've heard it's an amazing place for a holiday.'

'I've heard that too.'

Jock didn't think his tone gave anything away but the look Grace gave him said otherwise.

'It's given you itchy feet, hasn't it? To go somewhere new for more than just a holiday?'

And there it was again. An offering from the universe. A signpost to his escape route. How ironic was it that it was Grace who was presenting the opportunity to take a gentle first step towards that escape and to do it in a way that could protect them both?

'You could be right about that.' Jock tried to keep his tone merely thoughtful. 'There are still so many more places in the world I haven't seen. More adventures to be had.'

Okay…he might have caught a flicker of dismay in Grace's gaze but it was hard to tell because she broke the eye contact so swiftly.

'I'd better get going,' she said. 'I've got a wee adventure myself this afternoon. I'm taking a water taxi out for a home visit to Tessa to see how she's going, setting up for the twins.'

'Remind me where she lives?'

'Kumutoto Bay. She's got a waterfront property with its own jetty.'

'Ah… I believe that's one of the arms of Double Bay in the Queen Charlotte Sound. It's a beautiful spot. Not too far away at all. No phone reception that I remember, though.'

'No. She has a five-minute climb on the hill behind the house to use her cell phone or get the internet. They've got a landline, though.'

'Tell her I'm looking forward to seeing her next week.' But Jock was frowning as he thought about the implications of an extra degree of isolation. 'I might see if I can persuade her to be admitted for a few days before her C-section is scheduled, just to be on the safe side. Maybe you could check she's got her hospital bag packed already.'

'Will do.' Grace was moving away already. 'Thanks for lunch. It must be my turn to make some dinner tonight.'

'Don't worry about me. I've heard there's a tropical low forming northeast of New Zealand in the Coral Sea that could head our way later this week and I should go and check how secure *Lassie*'s moorings are.'

Grace paused, her head turning and her expression surprised. 'But it looks as calm as a millpond out there. It's not going to get rough while I'm going out to see Tessa, is it? I'm not sure I want to be out in big waves in a small boat.'

'It never gets really rough in the Sounds. It's out in Cook Strait that you get the gnarly seas with ten metre waves. And any bad weather with wind and rain will be days away yet and it could well be downgraded before it gets here. Don't worry.' He smiled at Grace, wanting to reassure her. 'The MetService is just tracking its formation and path. It could change direction or not be as severe as they think, but it's common sense to be prepared. Even if the water's not rough, strong gusts of wind can cause boats to come loose and move enough to get damaged.'

Grace smiled back. 'Good to know. Do you need any help with *Lassie*? I could meet you at the marina after work.'

'No...' The word came out with both a headshake and more emphasis than Jock had intended, but the prospect of being alone with Grace—in the very space where this had started getting out of control in the first place was something to be avoided at all costs.

'Thanks for the offer,' he added. 'But you'll be tired enough as it is after last night.' He turned away. 'It's not a problem. I can manage without you.'

Jock was running away, wasn't he?

Making sure nobody got too close to him.

Had he somehow sensed that Grace had stepped over the acceptable boundaries of friendship in how she felt about Jock?

Had it really happened that fast—in the few hours since that middle-of-the-night ultrasound on an unborn baby—or had Grace unknowingly been giving off signals earlier? Last night, perhaps, when she'd let herself think that it might be okay to join Mandy and Stefano on the dance floor and it would be acceptable to be that close to Jock? Because she'd been missing his touch so much since they'd called time on her sex-life experiment. So much that it was actually a physical pain.

No…it was more likely that he'd seen what she'd been thinking about as they'd shared a relieved smile when the ultrasound had suggested Maureen's baby wasn't in any immediate danger. Had he also seen what she hadn't quite realised herself at that point? That she could only imagine trying for another baby if it was going to be Jock's baby?

That she was head over heels in love with him?

No wonder the alarm had sounded and he was running, if that was the case. But was he so convinced that a long-term relationship and perhaps a family was the last thing he wanted that he was prepared to upend his entire life yet again and move to a new place—a new *country*—and start all over again?

She needed to fix this.

So that Jock didn't need to run away.

So that she could at least keep their friendship intact.

But, thanks to the fatigue that came from the sleepless night with Maureen, Grace couldn't think of what she should do. Did she need to step back and give Jock enough space to feel safe or would it be better to talk about it?

No...that fatigue also meant that it would be harder to avoid revealing, or even saying, something that would make things worse. Giving Jock space seemed like the only option, so Grace didn't fight the urge to crash that evening and she was sound asleep before Jock got home from checking on his boat.

She didn't see him at work at all the next day because he had a full theatre list and she had an antenatal clinic with a surprise twist when she discovered that the backache one of her mums was experiencing turned out to be the beginning of active labour. Grace was caught up with a delivery that lasted until the early hours of the next morning.

She slept late the next morning and walked to work under a moody sky that was grey with thickening clouds, responding to messages from Jenni, who was following weather reports in Australia and hoping the tropical storm that had now been upgraded to a cyclone was not going to affect her planned flight back to the UK.

She texted her back.

You'll be fine. Remember that the pilots want to get home as much as you do. They won't fly if it's not safe.

Have you heard what they've called it? Barry!!

No way!!

Grace sent a laughing face emoji, but she was starting to feel as grey as the clouds gathering above her head. Things were changing around her. Was the man who was quite possibly the love of her life moving rapidly away from her when a potentially damaging storm with the same name as her ex-husband was coming towards her?

She didn't want to be where she was right now. It felt like something was about to break.

Cyclone Barry was all everyone wanted to talk about at work that day, as they checked weather maps and forecasts. The ominous-looking circle of swirling cloud above the Tasman Sea was staying well away from the eastern coast of Australia, but it did keep tracking directly towards New Zealand and warnings were being issued about potentially very heavy rain and strong winds.

It was beginning to rain lightly that evening as Grace got home to find Jock was heading out to have a game of squash with Stefano. It was the first time they'd been face to face since he'd dropped the bombshell that he might be looking for a new life somewhere else.

'How did the visit with Tessa go yesterday?'

'Good. She's well set up with two of everything and a very supportive husband, Lawrence, who was there as well. He likes the idea of Tessa being admitted before the Caesarean. I asked if she had friends or family she could stay with in town if the weather got bad enough that it might cut them off, but she said she had too much to do at home to get ready for the babies.'

This was good, Grace thought. It was safe to talk about things like work and shared patients.

'Lawrence asked me if he should stay home himself from now on because his work takes him all over the district, but Tessa told him he'd drive her crazy if he was hanging around for more than a week watching for any signs she might be going into labour. He's taking a day off to come in for her next appointment with you, though.'

'What does he do?' Jock picked up his squash racquet that was leaning against the wall near the front door.

'I'm not sure. Something to do with the Department of Conservation, which means he spends time in the national parks. They're both really into nature. Their house is amazing—it's in the middle of a punga fern forest with a path that goes down the hill to a tiny sandy beach and the pier. The living room opens to a big deck which has the most beautiful view I've ever seen.'

It was safe to talk about nice views too.

Would it also be safe to talk about something more personal? Jock had the perfect excuse to escape if he needed to, with his squash racquet and car keys in one hand and holding the laces of a pair of trainers in the other.

'Did you hear from Jenni? Do you know if her flight took off? Last I heard, she was really worried about the cyclone.'

'Yes. Took off right on time. I'm following the flight on a tracking app.'

Grace bit her lip. 'Did you hear that they've named it Barry? My ex's name.'

Jock's expression was a sympathetic grimace as he nodded. His gaze not only met hers directly for the first time in this conversation, he held it. He was worried about how this might be affecting her, wasn't he?

He *cared* about her…and that gave Grace a squeeze around her heart that felt a lot like hope.

'It's quite an appropriate analogy really.' Grace took a deep breath. 'He's going to blow in, might do a bit of damage and then he'll disappear, never to be seen again.'

The corners of Jock's mouth curved upwards. 'I

like it,' he said quietly. 'And the sooner he's gone for good, the better.'

Grace couldn't look away as his gaze softened and then dropped to her lips. He was thinking about kissing her, wasn't he?

He *wanted* to kiss her.

She wanted him to.

She felt something else then, in the instant Jock jerked his gaze away from hers. A heartbeat of the kind of awkwardness they'd had before— after Jenni had jokingly suggested there could be something going on between them and the idea of being physically attracted to each other had been hanging in the air.

But this was worse because it was for a very different reason this time. It was because there *had* been something going on between them and...

And Grace's heart was breaking as she watched it fading into the distance because it was something Jock really, really didn't want. He couldn't get away fast enough right now, that was for sure. He muttered something about keeping Stefano waiting and then he was gone.

The first effects of Cyclone Barry began to be felt at the top of the South Island of New Zealand late the next afternoon, with heavy, squally rain showers and gusts of wind that were strong enough to be turning umbrellas inside out.

Jock was in the reception area of the labour ward when Grace went to file her patient notes.

'Sharon's ready for discharge,' she told the ward clerk. 'Baby number four has arrived with the minimum of fuss and she's keen to get back home before this weather gets any worse.'

'Aren't we all?' One of the registrars was shaking her head. 'I hear the river's rising quite fast. We might get stuck here ourselves.'

'Did you hear that the cyclone's been upgraded?' Someone else was scrolling a weather website. 'A cruise ship has cancelled a visit to Picton and there could well be disruptions to ferry crossings by this evening. It could be a category three, when or if it makes landfall.'

'When is that forecast for?' Jock was frowning. 'I hadn't heard that update. I'd better go and check on my boat again on my way home.'

One of the nurses shook her head. 'And this is the man who was just talking about some idyllic job opportunity in the Solomon Islands? You do know that's like the birthing suite for tropical cyclones, don't you?'

Grace caught her breath. Was Jock already searching for his next job? Talking to other people about it, but not to her? Was he thinking of going somewhere even more remote than Australia, like a group of islands in the South Pacific?

She handed over the patient notes. 'I need to go and help Sharon get sorted.'

What she really needed was to get away. As fast as Jock had when they'd been tempted to kiss each other last night.

She couldn't stop herself thinking about that the moment she walked through the door after fighting her way home through the wind and rain.

This wasn't going to work, was it?

The thought of being at home alone this evening while Jock was on board *Lassie*—the place he'd first made love to her—was almost unbearable.

He'd made it so very clear that he didn't need her. That he didn't want her as anything more than a friend.

She could hear the echo of his voice again.

As *if*...

Grace had known how he felt about commitment from before she'd even met Jock, so this was her problem, not his.

There might very well be no way of fixing this.

She had become everything he'd vowed to never have in his life, hadn't she? Someone who was in love with him and would marry him in a heartbeat if he asked.

Someone who wanted to have the baby he had sworn he would never bring into the world.

She was his worst nightmare, wasn't she?

The ringtone of her phone was a welcome interruption to the negative spiral her thoughts were threatening to develop into. Until she answered the call.

'Grace…? I need you…'

'*Tessa?* What's wrong?'

'I think I'm getting contractions.'

The hairs on the back of Grace's neck prickled. 'How often?'

'I've only had two. One was about fifteen minutes ago and I just got another one while I was climbing up the hill. It doesn't hurt but… I'm scared…'

'Where's Lawrence?'

'He was at work…the Pelorus Bridge Reserve…' The phone line was crackling. Fading in and out. '…been a slip on the main road and he's stuck…'

'Is there anyone who can bring you in to the hospital?'

'No… I tried…but…' Her words were cut off. The next ones were an agonised wail. '…all my fault…'

'Go back inside and stay dry and warm.' Grace raised her voice in the hope that Tessa might still be able to hear her. 'I'm onto it. I'll get hold of the coastguard. We'll come and get you as soon as we can…'

But Tessa didn't respond.

The only thing Grace could hear was the beeping sound of a disconnected call.

CHAPTER FOURTEEN

THERE WAS SOMETHING very disquieting about having no control over what was happening around you.

Jock didn't like the creaking and cracking sounds of boats bumping and scraping against their moorings as they rocked in the unsettled water beneath them and the gusts of wind that had seagulls shrieking as they battled the air currents in the fading daylight above.

There was nothing more he could do to make sure *Lassie* was securely tied up and nothing he could do if another boat came loose and created havoc. It was time to go home. He was hungry and the only thing on board the boat that was edible was a can of beans and he didn't want to heat that up because…

Because it would only make him remember being in the limited space of this tiny galley with Grace. Reaching past her to find a can opener and his arm brushing her skin. That look in her eyes when she told him how much she trusted him. When she asked him to make love to her...

Oh...*man*...

He could almost taste that first kiss all over again.

Could almost hear her voice. Calling him.

'Jock... *Jock*...are you there?'

Wait... He *could* hear her voice.

'Grace?' He walked out of the wheelhouse to look along the wooden pier. Yes, there she was, running towards him, a large backpack in her arms. 'What is it?'

'It's Tessa...' Grace was gasping for breath. 'She thinks she might be...going into labour. The coastguard's not...available...'

'No. I've been listening to the radio. There's a yacht in trouble at the entrance to the Sounds. And the tugboats are tied up trying to help get a ferry into port.'

'I can't find a water taxi...' Grace's gaze was fixed on his. 'I need to get to Tessa, Jock. She's all alone. And I can't get there by myself. I need *you*...'

He held his hands out. 'Give me the pack. Wait for me to help you on. There's enough of a swell to make movement unpredictable and I don't want you falling into the water.'

The pack was heavy. 'You've been *running* with this?'

'I drove to the hospital and then to the coast-guard buildings. I'm parked at the marina entrance.' Grace's grasp of his hand was tight as he helped her jump over a gap that suddenly widened between the side of the boat and the pier. 'But I did take the full home birth kit, just in case. It's got an oxygen cylinder and all the resuscitation gear, including fluids.'

'Good thinking,' Jock said. 'But let's hope we won't need it. Best-case scenario, we can look after Tessa, the coastguard will be able to get there and we can get her into hospital in time for that C-section.'

He let out a sigh of relief as *Lassie*'s engine started instantly. He jumped out of the boat then, unwinding the ropes he'd tied so firmly around the bollards. Seconds later, he was focusing on manoeuvring through gaps between other boats that were rolling in the swell.

'Put a life jacket on, Grace,' he ordered. 'And throw me one. It might be a bit gusty on the head of the arm before we turn into Kumutoto Bay. Do you think you'll be able to recognise Tessa's jetty?'

'Yes… If you can get into the bay, I can find it. The posts at the end are carved in a Māori design like a totem pole. They're very distinctive.'

The swell of the sea became more noticeable as they left the shelter of the marina. Jock could see how pale Grace's face was. Was she scared by the way the engine was surging as *Lassie* tipped and rolled in the dark sea water around them?

'We'll get there,' he promised. 'Just hang on.'

Grace nodded. 'I just know how Tessa's feeling,' she said. 'That this is *her* fault.'

'What? The cyclone? Going into labour?'

'Being trapped. Alone. Having herself and her babies in danger. She'll be thinking that she should have done something different, like coming to stay closer to the hospital. Or not talking her husband out of staying home with her. Even if it's not true, blaming yourself or someone else blaming you can destroy lives.'

Jock might be focusing on managing the roll of the boat as they sped out into the Sounds but he turned his head to give Grace an appalled look.

'Did *your* husband blame you?'

'I didn't do what he told me to do,' Grace admitted. 'I didn't stop work when he said I should. I wasn't eating the right food. I kept going to my yoga classes.'

Jock shook his head. 'He made you believe that you caused the death of your baby? He was gaslighting you, Grace—you do *know* that, don't you?'

She was staring through a windshield that had runnels of water streaming across it.

Like tears.

'I blamed myself, anyway, so what difference did it make?'

'Is that why you stayed in an abusive relationship for so long? Because you thought you deserved to be punished?' Jock's heart was breaking. 'Oh, Grace... You deserve so, so much more than that...'

He'd proved to her that she was capable of getting close enough to someone new to have an intimate relationship. But how did you make someone believe that they deserved to be loved? It would be like someone trying to tell him that he never needed to worry about not being good enough. That he would never hear anyone tell him ever again that he had ruined their life.

A larger swell brought *Lassie* down with a thump and Jock knew they were close to the head of the bay they were heading for. Grace was holding on for dear life now. She probably wouldn't even hear him if he tried to say anything more about how wrong her bastard of an ex-husband had been.

'It's okay.' He raised his voice to make sure he could be heard over the engine noise and the wind. 'I've got this. Trust me...'

Grace trusted Jock more than anyone else on earth, but that didn't stop this being beyond frightening. She could see that control of the boat wasn't easy and she was holding on for dear life as huge gusts of wind caught them before they could turn into the more sheltered area of the bay.

It was fraught trying to secure *Lassie* to Tessa's jetty as well, and Jock might have looked calm as he fought to keep the boat steady as Grace climbed off but she could tell how tense he was as her gaze caught his. They were going to need a lot more help from a team which was experienced in rescue scenarios to have any chance of getting a woman who was heavily pregnant with twins out of here and into the safe space of the hospital.

He caught Grace's hand and held it tightly to keep her upright in the wind and stinging sheets of rain as they got off the jetty and onto the steep steps that led up the hill to the house.

When they went into the house to find Tessa on her hands and knees on the floor, crying out with the pain of a contraction, it was obvious that they'd run out of time to get Tessa into hospital anyway. She was about to give birth right here.

'I can't do this,' Tessa sobbed. 'I'm too scared… What if something goes wrong? It will be all my fault…'

'That's *not* true.' Grace crouched on the floor to put her arms around Tessa. 'Don't even *think* like that.'

Jock was crouching beside her. He had the kit opened and took out a pair of sterile gloves to put on. 'I need to check what's happening down below, Tessa. Is it okay if I examine you?'

'Yes…of course.' But Tessa groaned as she lifted her head to focus on Grace. 'But this *is* my fault… If something happens to our babies, Lawrence will never forgive me… I'll never forgive *myself*…'

Grace could feel a bubble of something that felt horribly like panic developing inside her chest.

She could hear an echo of Jenni's voice in the back of her head, telling her the horror story of locked twins who'd been in the same positions as Tessa's unborn babies. Babies who could be in very real danger because of both their prematurity and their presentation.

Tessa wasn't the only one who was too scared to do this.

'You're fully dilated, Tessa,' Jock said. 'And I think we need to get ready to meet your babies.'

He looked up to meet Grace's gaze and she could see what he wasn't saying. Could he already feel the bottom of the breech twin emerging?

He knew just how emotionally involved Grace was in this case and that she understood only too well how Tessa was feeling. He held the eye contact long enough to not need any words. She could feel him gifting her his strength and the promise that he was going to do whatever he possibly could to give this dramatic birth story a happy ending.

But Tessa was sobbing. '*No*... It's not safe... Something's going to go wrong...'

'We've got this, Tessa,' Jock said calmly. 'You've instinctively chosen the best position to be in and the babies are still small enough for this to work. Grace, can you help set up?'

Moving helped. She got Tessa's clothing out of the way properly and put clean linen on the floor. Jock was getting out an infant resuscitation kit and IV gear. With another contraction starting, she rubbed Tessa's back and could feel herself tapping into Jock's confidence as she kept her voice calm and steady.

'You're doing so well, Tessa... Breathe in through your nose and out through your mouth. Keep your mouth soft and open and let the sound come out too.'

Tessa's outward sigh turned into a groan as it continued.

'I'm going to pop a wee needle in your hand when this contraction is over,' Jock told Tessa. 'Just in case we need to give you any medication or fluids.'

Grace felt the change in Jock's focus a moment later, however, before he had time to get an IV line in, and she could see why. The small buttocks of this first twin were appearing. Jock was very still, not touching the baby as he watched it appearing. Grace was watching him as she kept encouraging Tessa and breathing with her.

When the baby had appeared to the level of its umbilicus, Jock started moving. He hooked one finger under a leg and swept it sideways to bring it out. Then he swiftly did the same for the other leg. Half the baby could be seen now, dangling in mid-air. Grace reached to pass a towel to Jock and he wrapped it around the baby's lower body.

'I need to push,' Tessa groaned.

Jock was holding the baby with his thumbs on the lower back, ready to assist Tessa's pushing by applying gentle traction.

Grace was holding her breath. She tried to shut down a reminder of what could happen if the twins were caught on each other's chins, but she froze in what felt like a heart-stopping moment.

The small body slid out to the level of the shoulders and Grace watched the skill with which Jock turned the baby to deliver one arm and then rotated it gently right around to find the other shoulder and bring out the second arm. She saw him position his hands and knew he would be placing his fingers on the baby's face to tilt the head as it lay on his palm and forearm. He was using his other hand to grasp the shoulders and deliver the head and Grace couldn't let her breath out until that happened.

As she heard the first warbling cry of the tiny newborn girl, the frozen moment evaporated into a blur of movement.

'It's your first daughter,' Grace told Tessa. 'She's safe...'

'And she's perfect,' Jock added.

He was smiling at Grace. It wasn't the usual cheeky grin she'd come to love receiving from this man. This was a smile that was so soft it told her he understood how amazing this moment was. And that it was even more special to be sharing it with her?

She knew in that moment that she *was* important to Jock. That they had a connection that would be there for ever. That he might only ever love her as a friend but that love was something deep. And too precious to lose.

Grace picked up the bubble wrap and clean towels to keep the too small body warm and a suction bulb and oxygen, although the baby seemed to be breathing well and the APGAR score at five minutes was surprisingly good. Tessa turned so that she could see and touch her baby and Grace made a pile of cushions so she could lean back and hold her baby against her skin for extra warmth as they waited for the birth of the second twin.

Jock carefully palpated Tessa's abdomen to find the position the remaining baby was in. This time, when he made eye contact with Grace, he gave a single nod that came with a sigh of relief.

'Still cephalic,' he said quietly.

With more room suddenly available, the remaining baby could have moved into a different and more difficult presentation, but this second girl arrived in a textbook, headfirst delivery with even less fuss than her sister only thirty minutes later.

It took longer for the arrival of the skilled rescue teams that could get Tessa and her babies into hospital safely and the next hours were a blur of activity as they continued caring for Tessa, another rescue team was dispatched to find Lawrence and bring him to meet his daughters and a neonatal paediatrician was called in to assess the twins and decided they didn't need to be evacuated for specialist care.

Even Mother Nature seemed to be breathing a sigh of relief at the safe creation of this new family.

'Can you hear that?' Lawrence was holding one of his twins as Grace helped Tessa with her first breastfeeding of her babies.

'I can't hear a thing.' Tessa didn't look up. She was smiling down at her tiny, perfect daughter who was latching on like a champion.

'Exactly. The wind's stopped howling.'

'Cyclone Barry has apparently decided to move

back out to sea.' Jock was looking at his phone. 'He's gone. For good.'

He sent the ghost of a wink in Grace's direction. It wasn't just the cyclone with that name that would never be able to damage her life again, was it?

Thanks to Jock...

This wasn't the time to let that thought grow. It was helpful that the twin being held by her father started a shaky cry.

'Would you like to try feeding both babies at once, Tessa?'

'Oh, can I...?'

'Of course. I'll use these pillows to help support them.'

Lawrence let Grace take the second baby from his arms. 'I'm going to find my phone and get some photos of this,' he said.

'Oh...can you find those little hats my mum knitted for the girls? She'd be thrilled to see them wearing them.'

'Sure. Where's the bag with all the baby stuff in it?'

'It'll be with my bag.'

'I can't see that either.'

Grace groaned softly. 'Oh, *no*... I put those bags right by the door but that's the last time I saw them. With so many people there and everything that was happening to get you and the babies out of the house and into the coastguard boat, they must have been forgotten.'

Lawrence's face fell. 'I'll have to go and get them,' he said. But he looked as if it was the last thing he wanted to do. 'I don't want to leave you,' he told his wife. He reached out to touch one of the babies with a gentle rub. 'Or these little miracles.'

Jock glanced out of the window. 'It's nearly light,' he said. 'And it's so much calmer out there. I need to go and collect my boat, which is hopefully still tied up at your jetty, Tessa. I can bring your bags back.'

'I'll come with you,' Grace said. 'You've got this, Tessa, and you've got all the help you need just a bell press away here. It's time we left you and Lawrence to have some time alone together with these gorgeous daughters of yours. I can make sure we cleaned up properly after your home birth. And find anything extra you might think you need. That way, Lawrence won't need to be anywhere else for a while.' She raised her eyebrows as she turned to Jock. 'If that's okay with you?'

'No worries.' He didn't meet her gaze, however. He was busy with his phone. 'Let me see how soon I can find a water taxi to get us out there.'

CHAPTER FIFTEEN

IT WAS STILL the most beautiful view Grace had ever seen in her life.

She was standing on the deck of Tessa and Lawrence's home, looking out into Kumutoto Bay. Fronds of magnificent punga fern trees framed the view to an empty sea, with bush-covered hills in the distance. The water was still ruffled with the after-effects of the cyclone, but there were patches of blue between the clouds scooting across the morning sky and they felt like the promise of everything getting better.

Or almost everything…

Jock had taken the bags Tessa had packed down to put on board *Lassie* but she was waiting for him to come and tell her it was time to head back to town. She was hanging onto the last moments of being here in this amazing place.

Hanging onto what could be some of the last moments she ever had with Jock…?

Grace didn't turn around when she heard his footsteps on the wooden deck.

'I can't imagine choosing to leave all this behind,' she said quietly. 'It's paradise.'

'You don't have to,' Jock said.

'Neither do you.'

He came to stand beside her at the edge of the deck, putting his hands on the railing. 'I *will* miss it,' he said.

'I'll miss *you*.' Grace's voice was no more than a whisper.

'You'll be fine.' She could hear the smile in Jock's voice. 'Trust me.'

That made Grace turn her head sharply. 'Do you have any idea how often you say that?' She pulled in a breath. 'Trust is important to you, isn't it?'

Jock didn't hesitate in his response. 'It's everything,' he said.

'I *have* trusted you,' Grace said. 'More than I could ever trust anyone else.'

She swallowed hard. She had to say this, while she still had the chance. 'I trusted you to touch me,' she said softly. 'And I've never properly said thank you for what you gave me.'

Jock was staring out at the bay. 'You don't need to.' He flicked her a glance. Half a smile. 'It was my pleasure, believe me.'

Grace didn't return the smile. 'You gave me back a part of my life that I never thought I'd have again. No one else could have done that. I trusted you enough to let you touch me. I trusted you enough to fall in love with you, but you know that, don't you? That's why you're leaving…'

'Oh… *Grace*…' The low rumble of Jock's voice was almost a groan.

'I know you told me not to give up on my dreams and that I just needed to find the right person, and that person could never be you but…' Grace caught and held Jock's gaze. 'It *is* you, Jock McKay. It could never be anyone else.'

Jock closed his eyes. As if her words were visible and not seeing them could make them stop. But Grace couldn't stop. She loved Jock too much not to try and help him see something else he had been shutting out his entire life.

'You and Jenni are so alike,' she told him. 'You both think home is about a place. Jenni said it's the place where you feel properly safe and I get that. It's not something either of you had when you were growing up. Jenni's trying to make it about the place you grew up, but you're still looking for a place where you can feel that safe but, you know what? Home is bigger than just a place…it might not even *be* a place.'

Grace could hear the catch in her own voice. 'What if it's a *person*? What if all you need is the ability to trust that person?' She had to swallow the lump in her throat. 'What if you can never find your home because you can't give someone your trust?'

Jock's eyes were open again. His gaze locked onto hers.

'I trusted you, Jock,' Grace whispered. 'But you can't trust me and…it breaks my heart. And you're going to leave and maybe it's because you want to trust me but you're not going to let yourself and…and you leaving might very well break my world.' Her breath came out in something like a huff of laughter. 'I know you said you could never take the risk of building your world around someone else, but what do you do if that person *is* your world? What then?'

There was nothing he could do other than fold Grace into his arms.

And hold her.

Like he had that time when she'd told him about losing her baby. When he'd offered to push her off the boat.

When he'd held her in his arms again later than night and made love to her.

Every word she'd just said to him was true, wasn't it?

She'd trusted him so completely and he'd taken that gift, but he'd never had the courage or decency to give *his* trust to her. She deserved so much more than that.

'I'm so sorry,' he murmured against Grace's ear. 'I do run. I get scared and I run. Whenever I think someone might be getting close enough to discover the truth.'

'Which is?'

'That…' Jock struggled to find the words to something he'd never confessed aloud. 'That I'm not good enough. That if they're around long enough, they're going to find that out and it might ruin their life.'

'Oh, *Jock*…' Grace pulled back far enough to be able to look at him directly. And then she took her hands and put them on his face, cupping his chin in her palms. 'You could never ruin my life. You could only make it what I always dreamed it could be like if I was very, very lucky.'

Jock could see the tears sparkle in her eyes and then escape to roll down the side of her nose. 'You could never, ever be not enough for me. You are just perfect being exactly who you are. Except for one thing…'

Jock had to clear his throat. 'What's that?'

'You can't trust me. You've given me back my life but you can't trust me with your heart. You can't love me…'

'I *do* love you…' As the words came out, Jock realised just how true they were. And it wasn't the kind of love that bonded you with a sibling or a close friend. This was bigger. So much bigger he couldn't even see the edges of where it started or finished.

He didn't need to be afraid to give this woman his heart, did he? To trust that it would always be safe with her.

'I'm scared of the wrong thing,' he said slowly. 'What I should be scared of is waking up to find that you're not in my life. I love you, Grace Collins. I'm *in* love with you and the only thing I want right now is…*this*…'

Jock lowered his head to place his lips on hers. He hadn't kissed her since before Jenni had arrived for her visit and…

…and he was never going to leave it that long again.

How had he believed that he could protect himself by escaping this kind of love?

He was home.

Because this was where his heart was.

Grace could feel that too, couldn't she?

He could taste it on her lips. Feel it in the way her heart was beating against his own.

But he still wanted to hear the words. Even if it meant this kiss had to be broken.

'I love you, Grace.'

'I love you too, Jock.'

It was Grace who broke the next kiss. Eventually…

'We're going to have to confess, aren't we?'

'To Jenni? Aye... And she's never going to speak to me again.'

'You might be surprised. Let's call her as soon as we get home. She might be as happy as we are.'

'No.' Jock shook his head. 'Not possible.'

Grace laughed. 'No. You're right.' She wrapped her arms around his neck. 'One more kiss before we go,' she said. 'Please?'

She didn't have to ask twice...

EPILOGUE

A few months later...

FINDING HIS SISTER on his doorstep was the last
thing Jock McKay had expected. As far as he'd
known, she hadn't set foot outside Glasgow since
her holiday in New Zealand and that was only a
few short months ago so he certainly wouldn't
have thought she'd make such a big trip again so
soon.

Jenni had a bunch of balloons and a carry bag
in one hand. She put down the suitcase so that
she could throw her other arm around her brother.

'*Surprise*... Happy Birthday, Jock.'

Jock hugged her back. 'And to you... But...you
haven't come all the way across the world to celebrate our birthday, have you?'

'Why not?'

'Well, it's rather a long way to come when I
hadn't even planned any kind of a party. We're in
a bit of mess, what with packing and stuff.'

'We can make our own party. I've got cake. And wine. Or we can go out to dinner.'

'Am I missing something?' Jock was genuinely puzzled. 'We've never made that big a deal out of our birthdays and it's not a milestone like turning forty or something.' He took Jenni's suitcase and led the way down the hall. 'Not that Dan celebrated when he turned forty recently, but he's not really a party kind of guy, I guess.'

Was it his imagination or did Jenni have an odd look on her face at the mention of Dan's name?

'Can I have the same room I had last time I was here? You don't have a houseful of new hospital employees, do you?'

'Yes. And no. And you do realise we're about to move into the house we've bought, don't you? Our settlement date is next week.'

'I know. Grace told me. And I've seen pictures of the house, which is absolutely gorgeous. Have you really got your own jetty?'

'We do. We're right on the waterfront but we have road access as well. Best of both worlds.'

'Are there dolphins?'

Jock grinned. 'Not resident, as far as I know.'

'Grace loves dolphins.'

'I know.' Jock could feel a smile softening his lips. And his heart. 'And otters. She loves otters a lot.'

'She loves *you* a lot.' Jenni was taking her shopping bag and the balloons towards the kitchen. 'You didn't fool me, you know. I totally knew that Grace had fallen in love. I said so, didn't I?'

'You did,' Jock conceded. 'But we didn't even know ourselves at that point. So you couldn't possibly have known.'

'I so did.' Jenni took a bottle of champagne out of the bag and handed it to Jock. 'Put this in the fridge, please.'

He shook his head. 'So why did you keep speaking to me, then? When I'd broken the rules.'

Jenni shrugged. 'Grace looked too happy. I didn't want to jinx anything.'

Jock watched a box come out of the bag.

'Mud cake,' Jenni told him. 'Your favourite. I got it in Wellington.'

'Are you going to tell me the real reason you've come back here? We could have shared a cake and a glass of wine on a video call.'

'Birthdays need celebrating,' Jenni insisted. 'And so does finding love.' She turned to Jock and her smile was misty. 'I'm so happy for you,' she said softly. 'I'm so happy for both of you. The two people I love most in the world in love with each other? What could possibly be better than that?' She looked over Jock's shoulder. 'Where *is* Grace?'

'Out on a home visit. Do you remember the last night you were here on your visit? When we had to abandon you to go and see the woman who'd been in a car accident?'

'And you left me with Dan.' Jenni's laugh sounded a little off-key. 'Yes, I remember.'

'Well, that's who Grace has been visiting this afternoon. Maureen. She went to full term with no further complications and she had a little boy. Oscar, she's called him.'

'And what about the twins that got born during that cyclone?'

'They're the cutest babies ever. I saw Tessa at her final postnatal check-up recently. Grace and I have been invited to their christening.'

'That's a bit special.'

'More than you know. It was on the deck of Tessa's house that I proposed to Grace—the day after the twins were born. The day we called you and confessed.'

'A story with a happy ending all round, then.'

'You're not wrong.' Jock could hear the front door of the house opening and then closing. He heard Grace walking down the hallway and the moment she paused when she spotted the suitcase just inside the door of the spare room. Moments later, she came into the kitchen and her jaw dropped.

'*Jenni*…what on earth are *you* doing here?'

'*Surprise…*' Jenni held out her arms and Grace met her halfway across the kitchen floor.

'It's our birthday,' Jock explained. 'Apparently, Jenni decided she needed to come and celebrate.'

'I know it's your birthday, my love.' Grace extracted herself from Jenni's embrace and came close to Jock. 'I have a present for you.' She stood on tiptoes and kissed him.

Jock could feel her whispering 'Happy Birthday' against his lips before he began kissing her back. Thoroughly enough for Jenni to make a sound of protest.

'I am *here*, you know.'

Jock just grinned at Grace as he pulled back. 'Nice present,' he murmured. 'Thank you.'

'That's not your present.' Grace laughed. 'You can have that later.' She turned back to Jenni. 'I can't believe you're here. To celebrate a birthday? It's the best surprise ever.'

'And happy endings.' Jenni nodded. 'I'm all about happy endings.'

'So are we.'

Jock waited until he caught Grace's gaze again and he could fall into how much love he could see in her eyes.

He knew she would be seeing a reflection of that love.

They both knew they were at the beginning of the best happy ending ever.

* * * * *

*Look out for the next story in the
A Tale of Two Midwives duet*

Miracle Twins to Heal Them

*And if you enjoyed this story,
check out these other great reads
from Alison Roberts*

**Therapy Pup to Heal the Surgeon
Forbidden Nights with the Paramedic
Rebel Doctor's Baby Surprise**

All available now!